The Uninvited

On the Road with the

Greatest Rock Band You Never Heard

By Steven Vance Taylor

HURN
PUBLICATIONS

To Mia, Dax and Kian
"My crowning achievement, it's easy to see..."

A Note to the Reader:

Look, it's a memoir, not a deposition.

This is *my truth*, which never deviates far from *the truth*, but *that truth* sometimes hides in a dense, 20-year-old fog. I would also like to point out that a few of the names have been changed to protect the un-litigated. But most drop with factual abandon, like anvils in a *Road Runner* cartoon, in complete disregard for the consequences.

I apologize in advance for any collateral damage.

If you need me, I'll just be over here cowering behind the First Amendment.

The Gnome's Assessment

"When I go down
I'm goin' down in flames
Like Captain Kirk
Saving the world again"
-Down in Flames, The Uninvited

Summer, 1998:

"Statistically speaking, and I'm talkin' science here, it's mathematically impossible for you to be any more fucked than you are right now," says The Gnome. He had a penchant for annoyance unmatched by ordinary garden statuary.

Perpetually reclining on the dashboard, I imagine grabbing him by his stubby little pipe and chucking him out the van window, a smile of satisfaction spreading across my face as his plaster-of-Paris body explodes in a white plume of dust and ceramic shards in the rearview mirror. Chew on that, green pants.

Unfortunately, he's not mine to destroy.

"In a way it's good news," he continues. *"I mean you really hit bottom, right? A fatal aneurysm right now would be an improvement to your current situation."*

A blaring green and white road sign brings more bad news: 70 miles to Tulsa. I choke down the urge to heave up my oatmeal and ease the accelerator down another quarter inch, bringing the van from 85 to a nice round 90 mph. The U-Haul trailer responds with a little shimmy, like the last drunk in a conga line.

Encased in that trailer is the sum total of the band's worldly possessions and the irreplaceable tools of our trade. It's rated for a maximum speed of 55 mph, which is a little unsettling, but if we don't make Tulsa in the next 15 minutes The Gnome's assessment of our current status will be an understatement.

The sweat of my palms makes the wheel slippery in my hands.

I contemplate the eight other hands that grip this steering wheel daily, what they have done and where they have been, and my stomach does another turn. The bacterial smorgasbord that germinates on this circular Petri dish is probably sprouting the next worldwide pandemic.

Though I often forget, I actually love the people connected to those hands. They are my brothers-in-arms sharing my greatest and most tragic moments. We are joined spiritually and contractually just like any marriage. Which means The Van is just a freakish rolling polygamist compound. How long can crabs survive on an unwashed surface? Visions of 6th grade Sex Ed horror movies play in my head.

It's week four of the measly four weeks of promotion Atlantic Records is giving us for our first-ever major label single, "What God Said;" a ska-seasoned post-punk diatribe that takes a shot at explaining the meaning of life in three minutes and 30 seconds.

It's essential to the inner workings of the music business to categorize bands with one-word labels, ostensibly so people know if your record matches their wardrobe. Folks with tie-die regalia listen to "Psychedelic" bands like the Grateful Dead or Phish. The leather-and-studs crowd obviously prefer "Metal," the mohawks like "Punk," and so on.

Our crowd is the jeans and graphic t-shirt type, strategically torn and perhaps accessorized with a flannel—the uniform of "Alternative." The label is applied as a variation of plain ol' "Rock", whose followers might swap out the flannel with a leather jacket and are less likely to sport a tongue piercing.

Today the song is number three at the highest rated radio station in Oklahoma and we are screaming down Highway 44 to make our gig at the station's massive K-ROCK festival. At the end of this highway 20,000 people are deep in the process of rocking their asses off.

We're up next ... in 15 minutes.

Not only is this the biggest gig of the tour, it's supposed to be the turning point of our career. 10 years from now, when "Behind the Music" chronicles our meteoric rise to rock godliness, this gig is supposed to be the watershed moment when we transition from unknowns to chart-topping mega-sensation-media-darlings.

Tragedy is supposed to strike way after success, *then* we overcome insurmountable odds to reclaim our rightful place in the rock pantheon. That's the traditional career path and *by God* we are NOT about to deviate from the norm.

The word from the suits was clear: if we push the single to number one in Tulsa, the promotion dollars from Atlantic will continue to flow. If not, the record dies along with every hope, dream, and ambition we have starved and bled for over the last eight years. Blowing the gig is NOT on the agenda.

I push the accelerator down the last eighth-inch to the unyielding steel floor while casting a surreptitious glance at T-Money in the passenger seat. In place of the expected Raised Eyebrow of Disapproval is the ashen pallor of a face completely devoid of blood. T-Money, aka Our Man Tony, might just die of internal self-flagellation. That's fine. Right now, I would pull his still-beating heart from his chest if I didn't think it would have a negative impact on our friendship.

Three hours earlier we had left our bowls of half-eaten oatmeal, piled in the van, and proceeded to take a left out of the Waffle House parking lot secure in the knowledge that our capable, steadfast, and trusty road manager, T-Money, had the situation in hand.

Tony started working for the band eight years earlier, sometime around our first gig. He just appeared on stage after the show asking if we needed a hand loading out the gear. Loading, unloading, hauling or moving equipment—amps, drums, road cases—is back breaking drudgery that sucks the fun juice out of any musical endeavor. Tony's offer was gratefully accepted.

Show after show, month after month, Tony showed up to help load in and load out. Soon, he was running the merch booth, selling CD's, copying set lists, changing strings, organizing beer runs, and fixing anything and everything with his omnipresent duct tape until finally, T-Money, Our Man Tony, became indispensable.

Strangely, he asked for nothing in return, at least not monetary compensation. Tony wasn't in it for fame-by-association, nor did we ever walk in on him snorting blow off a groupie's ass. Tony, quite simply, loved the music. The songs, the lyrics, the harmonies, the musicianship—Tony was quite possibly our biggest fan.

But right now he was our biggest asshole—not counting The Gnome of course. As Chief Navigator, T-Money plans every route, meal, pee stop, and smoke break down to the second with cool and calculated Spock-like efficiency. When we pulled out of that Waffle House, T-Money said go left so that's what we did. Unquestioningly. Because T-Money said so.

117 miles later, with a splayed highway map in his lap, Our Man Tony became visibly anxious. It was getting close to load-in time and I asked which exit I should be looking for. Glancing from his map to passing road signs I could see him slowly losing his typical self-assured poise until an audible gulping sound emanated from his constricted throat.

"Um, uh, guys, uh, we're uh, going in the wrong direction. We have to turn around. Now."

Like the Five Stages of Death we started with Denial.

"Impossible!"

"No way"

"Bullshit!"

Then we moved quickly to Anger.

"What the FUCK? We're supposed to be at the gig in 15 MINUTES!"

The other three stages, Bargaining, Depression and Acceptance, were still a long way off. Especially Acceptance.

Derision, apologies, panic, and incredulity were all present and accounted for, until icy tense silence took over, broken occasionally by commentary from The Gnome.

"You still have that Pope hat from Hotdog On A Stick ... No one could drop a basket of corn dogs into a deep fryer quite like the Stevester ... Free corn dogs means never going hungry."

I grind my teeth and lean in toward the wheel. *Don't engage The Gnome ... Don't engage The Gnome...*

I should have left the smirking bastard on my neighbor's porch. At the time, I thought it would be so hilarious to kidnap The Gnome. I didn't know the old couple whose lawn he watched over day and night. They had him lying on a tiny bench along with a gigantic dragonfly whose colossal translucent wings gave a primordial vibe to an otherwise pastoral suburban setting.

My plan was to nab The Gnome and take pictures of him at various landmarks around the country, then send the Polaroid snapshots back to the elderly couple every few days.

After grabbing him I left the following note on his little bench:

... Dear Family,

This notice is to inform you that Section C-6154 of the Helsinki International Lawn Gnome Accord of 1956 entitles me to two weeks vacation every year. As you may recall, the HILG Accord was written following the Lawn Gnome Uprising of '52 and helped put an end to the very unpleasant Pink Flamingo Hostage Crisis of '55. Thanks to the HILG Accord, Lawn Gnomes have been peacefully watching suburban grass grow for 45 years.

But as nice as this lawn is, I'm getting a little tired and need some time off.

See you soon—
Jazz Hands
Your Lawn Gnome

Everything was going fine in the first few days of the tour, but we didn't hit any actual "landmarks." In lieu of recognizable National Icons we got a nice shot of The Gnome on top of a urinal at a truck stop outside of Fresno, and another in the parking lot being kissed by a prostitute. We gave her $3.36 in change from the van ash tray, and she seemed vaguely pleased that was all we wanted. But somewhere around Los Angeles, The Gnome became, quite simply, an insufferable prick.

"Reach over, open the door, and give him a shove," says The Gnome as I eye T-Money and his thousand-mile stare.

Shut up, I reply in my head. *The next picture I take of you will feature nothing but your feet hanging out of a cow's ass.*

The Gnome just laughs, delighted that I am playing along. I am about to elaborate on other plans I have for his destruction when the cell phone rings.

Tony pulls out the brick-like device, checks the display, and looks at me with even deeper concern. "It's Braveheart," he says.

That would be Hamish MacNiven, our perpetually angry Scottish manager.

I give a slight nod, which means go ahead and answer the phone even though the roaming charges on the call will cost more than all the money we are going to make from today's gig—if there is a gig today.

He flips open the brick, pulls out a foot of antenna, stretches it out the window into the Oklahoma dust and says, "Tony here."

Despite the road noise of an un-insulated steel van roaring down the highway at 100mph the ensuing torrent of Scottish obscenities is clearly audible: "...fa fawk sake ya dahft bastards..."

T-Money makes a few plaintive attempts to inject a line or two of hesitant explanation, but it's clear that Braveheart isn't into it. Tony's side of the conversation dwindles down to: "Sorry ... Sorry ... Yes ... We are breaking every speed law ... Okay ... Sorry ... Okay..." He folds up the brick and unconsciously pushes down the antenna.

My bandmates, JT, Bill, and Bruce all push their heads into the space between the driver and passenger seat eager to hear if our career is retrievable from the currently flushing toilet.

"They are going to push Verve Pipe into our slot," T-Money says to the front windshield. "If we get there before Third Eye Blind takes the stage, they'll try to squeeze us in but after that we're hosed. That buys us 40 minutes."

Bill, Bruce and JT sink slowly back into their seats, each lost in their own inner meltdown.

I wonder if The Gnome is giving them shit.

Motivated by fear, I rummage around the dark back closet of my brain, conjuring up the forgotten lessons of my high school physics class. Time equals distance divided by rate. At our current velocity we will just barely ... not make it. I try to push the pedal further but it's already lying on the floor. Frustration contracts every single muscle in my body simultaneously, but with extreme effort and controlled breathing I manage to release them one at a time, starting with my eyebrows and working my way down.

Keeping to the fast lane we pass semis like they are parked on the side of the road. I whisper a silent prayer asking that Mr. Highway Patrolman might linger over an extra Bear Claw this morning, when I realize something else is wrong. A vague melancholy, unrelated to the current crisis, is slowly filling the van, ethereal and intangible.

I take a quick inventory of my senses and realize the problem is coming from an unlikely source: the stereo. Last night in Amarillo we swapped CDs with the opening band in accordance with long standing tradition. I can't remember their name, but I do recall some kind of mopey black-haired Emocore outfit whose droning monotone drove me across the street for a burrito. Bill must have slipped in their disc before we left the motel this morning.

What many people don't know is that the style of music called "Emo"—roughly taken from the word "Emotional"—was originally developed by Warner Brothers Music as an alternate means of euthanizing cattle before the slaughter; the thought being that hitting them over the head with an iron mallet was inhumane.

Following thorough research, however, the National Cattle Association decided that no living creature should suffer the torment of being literally bored to death, and they enthusiastically returned to the use of the mallet. Warner Bros., facing a potential loss of millions in R&D costs, went ahead and released their Emocore records and bands to consumers worldwide heedless of the consequences to public health and safety.

I stab the eject button so hard I stub my thumb. Cursing and shaking my hand I ask JT, my little brother and life-long musical co-conspirator, if we have anything uplifting since "...this dismal dreck makes me want to swerve into on-coming traffic." JT reaches into the CD box and pulls out a disc by our good friends The Young Dubliners. A moment later their high-octane party jig rock has our five heads bobbing in unison, allowing the slightest air of Celtic optimism to creep into the atmosphere. Unfortunately, somewhere around the second chorus of "Rocky Road to Dublin" the spell is broken by a low moan emanating from the rear of the van. T-Money shuts off the stereo and shushes everyone. We all listen intently to the mysterious sound, glancing around at each other with "what the hell?" expressions.

"It's the differential," says Bruce.

"Wheel bearings," chimes Bill.

"I think the right trailer wheel is smoking," says JT looking out the back window. "Isn't there some kind of giant yellow warning sign on the side of that thing saying something about 55mph ... blah, blah, blah?"

"We are all going to die," says The Gnome.

"Shall I pull over?" I ask.

The van falls silent save for the trailer's sustained death wail.

"I say let it burn," JT announces.

A wave of somber agreement ripples through the van and my

gas foot remains cemented to the floor. The Gnome goes on about twisted steel and fiery death, but I pay no attention.

Reaching over to the center console drink holder I grab the ubiquitous tin of Altoids, flip it open with a practiced thumb, and pour one-third of the contents into my mouth. A vigorous chewing releases the desired peppermint supernova. I toss the tin back in the drink holder, dig out a can of Red Bull from the cooler between the seats, and wash down the residual masticated powder. BAM! The cocaine-like rush is upon me. Not only are my senses heightened to peak performance, I am now sporting the freshest breath in all of Oklahoma.

Traffic increases as we near the outskirts of the city. No matter. My confidence bolstered by taurine and peppermint oil, I weave the van and trailer in and out of the gaps between the slower moving vehicles despite the ever-decreasing clearances.

Brake lights flash.

Horns honk.

The Gnome freaks out.

Even my bandmates let go the occasional gasp.

A quick glance in the right rearview reveals discernible smoke emanating from the right rear trailer tire—JT was right; that can't be a good sign. No matter. There's a dying career in this van and the only hope of resuscitation lies at the end of the 18th exit of this highway.

Off-ramp after off-ramp flashes by the passenger-side window though our speed has diminished somewhat due to the melting trailer axel.

Roadmap in hand, T-Money counts down the exits: "Four more to go ... three more to go..."

Finally, our road to redemption reveals itself in green and white, complete with a little reflective arrow pointing the way.

"Here!" Tony exclaims unnecessarily.

I weave the smoking, screaming van/trailer combo across

three lanes of traffic, cutting off a pickup truck with a small arsenal of rifles mounted in the rear window.

"Excuse me ... sorry ... musical emergency coming through," I mutter under my breath.

I ease my cramping gas foot for the stop sign at the end of the ramp, but JT says, "I don't think that applies to us," so we blow through it.

Our first break of the day: the festival grounds are right off the highway. We turn at the "Festival Parking" sign. An attendant steps out at the sight of the approaching van ready to extort the colossal parking fee—we don't have time. I reach into my back pocket, pull out a laminate from three shows ago, and hold it out the window like a cop badge, leaving the indignant attendant in a cloud of parking lot dust and acrid burning axel smoke.

"Excuse me ... sorry ...dying career emergency," I mutter with actual sincerity. Despite the urgency I regret the douchbagary and swallow down a pang of guilt. My karma will definitely require a thorough sanitizing.

JT spies the stage and a small dirt access road. "Over there," he says and points.

As I steer for the final stretch the axel seizes up completely, freezing the right rear tire. The trailer pulls hard to the right, threatening to jack-knife, but I compensate with a pull to the left determined to drag the trailer the last quarter mile to the stage.

A glance in the rear-view shows two guys in yellow security jackets coming up fast on ATVs. The amount of dust and smoke we're kicking into their faces will undoubtedly add some enthusiasm to our upcoming Apology Jubilee.

We round the corner to the backstage area and look for an opening among the massive tour busses and motor coaches of the Rock Star Aristocracy. Once again, I choke back the familiar bus envy. What's it going to take? For three years we've rolled around the country in this freakin' soup can. Will we ever experience the smooth glide of real shock absorbers?

"Wow, checkout the road palaces," says The Gnome. *"Those things have satellite TV, full gyms, comfy beds, wet bars ... I hear some of them even have stripper poles. But your van is cool. It's got a drink holder with some kind of sludge in the bottom ... and a cigarette lighter that used to really work."*

I limp the van between the pristine road yachts trying not to increase today's costly blowout with a massive white scratch down Bad Religion's bitchin custom paint job. Finally, with an exhausted sigh, we roll into what I assume is the load-in area.

A small man with a clipboard and tiny mustache approaches the van wearing the scowl of a person burdened with multi-million-dollar responsibility, left at the mercy of a hundred or so post-adolescent prima donnas.

"He looks pissed," says The Gnome.

"He looks pissed," I repeat out loud.

Mustache Guy steps up to the van window without taking his eyes off his clipboard. "The Uninvited, I presume."

"That's us," I say. "Are we good to load-in? Did we miss our slot?"

"Your wheel is on fire," he says.

"Um, yes, that's pretty high on the fix-it list. But I gotta tell ya, if you don't let us play, I might as well let the whole trailer burn to the ground."

Always Never Sucking

"Come shake the hand
Of the invisible man
My name is Nobody"
- Invisible Man, The Uninvited

Though I play guitar in The Uninvited, banjo was my first love.
Not the extra-Y-chromosome-marry-your-sister banjo, but the
cool beatnik banjo of my parents' generation.

Pete Seeger used the five-string as an instrument of joy and
protest, inspiring millions of soon-to-be-hippies to Dropout, Turn
On, and Fight the Power. Early espousals of the joys of "Free
Love" were delivered atop melodies provided by America's first
instrument. In the coffee shops of New York's Greenwich Village
and San Francisco's North Beach guys like Jack Kerouac and Allen
Ginsberg defined and chronicled the sweeping cultural upheavals
of the late 1950's, all while tapping their toes to some guy with a
goatee and beret laying it down on a banjo. And you can bet that
guy was getting himself some Free Love back behind the espresso
machine.

In addition, the instrument was a rarity. Growing up in San
Diego County, no one played the banjo. Its uniqueness appealed
to the nonconformist aspect of my nature. As a child I often ran
counter to what the cool kids were doing, which made me, in a
word, uncool. In junior high my uncool banjo and I were
inseparable. I practiced in the back of the bus on the way to
school. During recess I was plucking away under the bleachers. By
the end of junior high the banjo was completely intertwined with
my whole identity.

When I was in the 8th grade one of the most popular shows on
television was *The Gong Show*, a cheesy precursor to actual talent
shows like *American Idol*. Watching the show one evening I jotted

down the phone number that flashed at the end of every program: "If you would like to appear on *The Gong Show*, call this number..." First prize was $750.00—not the million-dollar record deal later offered by *American Idol*. But at the time $750 would buy a lot of banjo strings. I called the number and arranged for an audition in Hollywood in two weeks.

When Dad got home from work that night I poured him his traditional double bourbon. ("Hold all four fingers around the glass and pour to the last finger.") Dad had an upholstery shop that required every drop of his reserves for 16 hours a day. The man who came home nightly carried a weariness born of an overdeveloped work ethic.

I handed Dad the drink and waited impatiently. When the first sip was safely past his Adam's apple, I announced that I needed a ride to Hollywood—a 3-hour trip. My overworked dad swirled his drink with his finger while Mom watched him over her needlework. Dad didn't meet her stare, he didn't have to; he could feel it, an entire conversation taking place without words or expressions. But Mom always won.

He took a pull of his drink and studied the ice for a good 30 seconds before saying, "*The Gong Show*. Of course. Let's go."

All humility aside, nothing is more nauseatingly adorable than a 12-year-old banjo player in a black vest and bow tie. My guitar-playing friend, Rick, and I breezed through the auditions with pats on the head from grinning judges. The taping of the actual show, however, was a life-altering trip right down the rabbit hole. *The Gong Show* was a freak magnet, and I soon found out those were real freaks, not actors. In the green room, "The Unknown Comic," a guy with a perpetual lunch bag over his head, swore to himself while trying to stuff an oversized sandwich though a tiny mouth hole in his paper sack. On the other side of the room a mime in blackface sat in an invisible electric chair that apparently fired off every 30 seconds or so.

But at the top of the list was the mad-hatter himself, Chuck

Barris, the show's producer and host. Barris was quirky and fun when the cameras were rolling, quirky and angry when they weren't. Up until the moment I met Mr. Barris I had no idea that the word "fuck" could comprise 90% of the content of every sentence—

"Fuck, I can't fucking believe that fucking fuck fucked me so hard. Fuck!"

During rehearsal he would sprinkle a few words of direction in between long streams of expletives, then go back to a side-stage table where he sat between two of the most beautiful women I had ever seen in my young life. I watched as he nuzzled the neck of one girl while his unseen hand made the other girl squirm and giggle.

My body had just started producing testosterone by the gallon and the mesmerizing scene made me think I could get used to this whole showbiz thing. (*Years later Chuck Barris would claim that he killed 33 people while working for the CIA, an assertion the CIA denies. It doesn't really matter whether he did or not. Just making the claim showed he was wonderfully bat-shit crazy and somehow endeared him to me even more*).

The taping of the show was at 7:00pm in front of a live studio audience. Behind the curtain a production assistant wearing a headset reminiscent of the ones used by the Apollo astronauts guided us to our mark. We stood facing the back of the curtain listening to the audience roar as a housewife in a giant cereal box was "gonged" while juggling four slices of buttered toast. *No one can see you cry inside a box of Cocoa Crispies,* I thought to myself.

As I stood staring at the backside of the dark fabric of the curtain, I experienced the first nervous breakdown of my 12 years of life. Why was I here? What in the hell was I doing? I am about to make a gigantic ass of myself on nationwide television. All my friends and family will see me flail ineffectively for a few seconds before I'm booed into humiliation and banished from society forever. I will never have a girlfriend. I will never get laid. Ever.

Without warning the velvet wall rose to the auditory assault of the crowd and blinding stage lights. Giant rolling television cameras with lenses like howitzers closed in. I remember thinking I had two choices: I could projectile vomit all over the set like a gastronomic lawn sprinkler, or I could start playing this banjo that hung from my shoulder...

I chose the latter.

Barris had decided to alter our act. About halfway through our song he had a 300-pound baby in diapers, Abraham Lincoln, a guy on a unicycle, and "The Unknown Comic" dance spasmodically around us in a circle. Apparently, an epileptic Abraham Lincoln did little to increase our appeal. The B-list celebrity panel, refugees from cancelled sit-coms, sat distractedly staring into space, most likely contemplating the humiliating set of circumstances that led them to this bizarre moment.

In the end we did not get "gonged," but we didn't win the $750 grand prize either. I left the studio that evening with a crock pot under my arm—the obligatory "lovely parting gift"—and a valuable lesson: If left unchecked the Entertainment Business will ruthlessly, relentlessly, and unconscionably bend you over to serve its own ends. This would not be the last Spasmodic Lincoln "Show Biz" would throw at us.

But *The Gong Show* experience yielded much more than kitchen appliances and valuable lessons, it sparked a musical partnership that would last my entire life. My younger brother, JT, was sitting in the audience that night enamored by the entire circus and my newly acquired pre-adolescent celebrity. He wanted in.

Using nothing but a library book and a stack of vinyl records, he taught himself how to play the mandolin with an eye toward being a part of whatever this was. Amazingly, within a few weeks he was a full-on mandolin shredder. Without the guidance of a music teacher, JT had developed his own twisted playing style. The stack of records he used in his vinyl mentorship included not only bluegrass legend Bill Monroe, but Black Sabbath and Pink Floyd as well. If Jimi Hendrix played the mandolin, he would have sounded a lot like JT.

And there was something else to my little brother besides near-prodigy musical ability. Whatever mystical element creates attraction—aura, vibration, empathy, or pixie dust—JT's pockets were full of it. He had a way of making people feel like they were reuniting with a long-lost friend when meeting him for the first time. An easy confidence, sharp intellect, and quick wit created a broad and enduring circle of friends and admirers. He partied with the best of them, yet still maintained a straight-A report card. Anything he put his hand to—drama, music, Zen meditation —was instantly second nature to him. Ferris Bueller wishes he was JT.

In this lifetime, if you are lucky, the Universe will put a small handful of extraordinary people in your path. For me, I am eternally grateful to whatever powers the cosmos that JT followed me into this world.

Throughout junior high and high school my brother and I were obsessed with music. We learned to harmonize in that singular fashion that only brothers can achieve. When we stepped up to the mic, sun beams flared, rainbows formed, puppies played in flowery meadows. Better yet, the effect seemed to impair the visual acumen of females, because girls gave us a lot more attention than our average looks would have otherwise garnered.

Music was manna from the gods.

After high school, like all good children of suburbia, we ran off to college to learn to be responsible cogs in America's gigantic widget-producing machinery. But making widgets wasn't nearly as fun as making music. Within two years of graduating college, I landed back on my little brother's couch in Los Angeles, paying rent with a weekly bag of groceries. We started jamming on brand new electric guitars, purchased with paychecks from making widgets.

For us, the transition from acoustic instruments to electric guitars was the equivalent of parking your tricycle and jumping on a Harley Davidson. The power was intoxicating. Distortion, glass-shattering volume, notes that sustain for days – cranial neurons firing electric impulses down neural pathways to activate phalanges against strings that in turn create new electric impulses traveling at light-speed through a quarter-inch instrument cable straight into a 100-watt amplifier and ending in a blasting 120 disciple harmonic translation of that original synaptic connection. Playing electric guitar was a transforming experience, like growing another mouth, only much louder, and capable of saying things that your original mouth could never utter.

We made all this noise in a dilapidated wreck across the street from the University of Southern California where JT had just graduated. Ten years earlier the structure could have been described as a house, but now it was just a conglomeration of loosely attached two-by-fours and stucco waiting for a euthanizing bulldozer. All that commotion, of course, attracted other noise makers. Within weeks of our electric guitar procurement, we had three fellow occupiers of The Wreck, who also doubled as our bandmates in what became our very first rock band, The Bogartz.

The unrestrained volume of our rehearsals was audible on campus, so it wasn't long until the inebriated contingent of academia stumbled over to see what all the hub-bub was about. Soon the house was not only the band's residence, it was also our main venue. We were the house band at our own house. We even built a stage in the back yard out of stolen milk crates. Every time the cops shut us down we were standing on $34,000 in fines and a cumulative prison sentence of about 12 years.

In the grand tradition of our rock and roll forefathers, our parties became epic extravaganzas of excess. Every Saturday night turned into a re-run of Caligula's bachelor party. People came from miles around to dance, drink, puke, fight, fuck, and generally get out of control while we provided the soundtrack.

But there was one minor drawback to all the depraved fun: the band sucked. Granted, a little sucking never stood in the way of a typical rock band's success, but we *really* sucked. We sucked so hard the barometric pressure of the entire city of Los Angeles would drop every time we hit the stage. Walls would buckle inwards. People would have trouble breathing. No vacuum cleaner ever built could suck as hard as we did.

We stank.

We knew it.

We didn't care.

Until one day I woke up, and suddenly, I cared. Standing in a quarter-inch deep beer lake that covered the entire living room floor I realized that music, the fuel of my soul, had been drowning for two years in tequila and bong water. Music had defined my being since the 6th grade, so what was I if not a musician? And what do musicians do? They fucking make music.

I walked over to the mattress which vaguely supported my brother's six-foot-six frame. His head and feet hung at odd angles from each end of the ancient twin. I gave him a nudge with my big toe.

"Hey," I announced, "it's time to stop sucking. Let's go form a real band."

And thus, The Uninvited was born.

With the hangover of The Bogartz a fuzzy memory, we were determined that the new band would not suck. The first person to "audition" for our suck-free endeavor was bassist, Bill Cory. The title "bassist," however, was loosely applied, meaning that Bill neither played nor owned an actual bass. What he did possess was an overgrown blond Mohawk that flopped over the shaved sides of his head giving him a unique, surfer-rock-dude look that would lend a touch of street cred to any album cover. Still, we were reluctant to bring him on board since looking like you don't suck is not quite the same as actually not sucking.

Bill was fan of the Bogartz, and when he heard we were forming a new band he wanted in. Badly. I suspect he was more motivated by the swirling party vortex surrounding the Bogartz than the musical acumen of the five college students on mushrooms and vodka playing five different songs all at the same time. Regardless, Bill's unrelenting persistence wore us down.

"I can play bar chords on a guitar."

"That's not a bass."

"The top four strings are tuned the same. How hard can it be?"

"It's hard. Otherwise, everyone would play bass."

"I'll take lessons."

"How? You don't even own a bass."

"Okay, I'll take next semester's tuition money and I'll buy a brand new Fender P-Bass, a 500 watt amp and two speaker cabinets loaded with 18 inch subs."

"Hmm. Sounds like a cool rig. But how will you pay for school?"

"If we're going to be rock stars why do I need to go to college?"

"Congratulations, you're our new bass player."

Shortly after Bill pledged his last dime to the project, we found drummer Bruce Logan. A full-time professional musician, Bruce had recently arrived in LA and was willing to hitch his wagon to ours as long as we were committed to going all the way. Raised on John Bonham yet finished on Buddy Miles, Bruce was the Musician of the band, scribbling notes on charts as the songs took shape, all the while explaining to Bill—to the point of annoyance—that bass and drums were really a single instrument.

The game plan moving forward was to achieve the Bruce Level of Not Sucking before we would play a single gig. It took about a year, but in that lap around the sun, Bill and Bruce melded into a thunder-pumping apparatus of subsonic euphoria. Bruce got the bass player of his dreams while Bill's chops rose to the promise of his hair.

Another reason it took a full year before we played our first gig was that we had to wait for Bill to turn 21. In the State of California, you can sign up to die for your country at 18, you can cast a vote for the most powerful office in the world, but Jesus and the Judge will both condemn you for defiling your liver with a fermented grain beverage before the age of 21. Since alcohol is rock's favorite garnish, every club in the city required an ID certifying that you were old enough to make poor life choices.

Thus, on Bill's 21st birthday we took a band field trip to the legendary Whiskey A Go-Go to celebrate his coming-of-age in an atmosphere rich in hair extensions and chrome studs. I loved the Whiskey, but like most Hollywood legends 20-years past their prime and steeped in alcohol, it wasn't wearing its age very well. At some point they simply gave up on the interior and painted everything black, making it impossible to imagine that psychedelic mini-skirts and white patent leather boots once lit up the dance floor. But the dark, seedy mood brought out the androgynous vampires in droves, each one hoping to be the next Jim Morrison, Perry Ferrill, or Axl Rose, all of whom once graced that very stage.

Bill proudly displayed his license to a doorman who didn't look at it, and we pushed our way through spandex and leather to the bar. I smiled to myself, realizing we were the weird ones in our plain jeans and t-shirts, but we simply would not/could not pull off the zebra-stripe-spandex-and-cowboy-boots look that choked the scene on Hollywood Blvd.

I placed my hand on our bass player's shoulder and said, "Let me introduce you to my good friend, Jack Daniels."

Later on I realized that this statement was ill-conceived, poorly timed, and completely unfactual. Not only was Jack Daniels not a friend of mine, he's a complete asshole who shouldn't be introduced to anyone, especially young impressionable bass players partaking in their first rock 'n roll baptism.

Regardless, Bill and Jack got along swimmingly.

The bartender poured shot after shot while JT's credit card sat in a small glass behind the bar. After four or five rounds a very large gentleman in a black shirt emblazoned with the word "Security" stepped up to the four of us.

"The bank said I have to do this in your presence." Holding JT's credit card in one hand and a pair of scissors in the other he proceeded to make a small pile of plastic confetti on the bar. "Now how are you paying for these drinks?"

I fumble for my wallet and finally produce another piece of plastic despite a certain skepticism regarding its own potency.

Two minutes later he slides it back across the bar. "Nope."

JT confidently assures the bouncer that there's no problem here, taking out his last piece of plastic, which ultimately results in yet another small pile of confetti.

Things get hazy at this point. I recall that my girlfriend showed up, whispering ideas about whip cream that eventually lured me from the club and back to the band's apartment. Later that evening, around 3 a.m., I was rummaging through the fridge cursing an empty can of Cool Whip when JT and his girlfriend, Eris, came floundering through the door.

Looking up I noticed something missing. "Hey Bro," I said, "Where's Bill?"

"I thought he was with you," says JT.

Oh shit.

Brothers-in-arms never leave a man behind, and that is exactly what we did. With a surge of panic I hastily tie my bathrobe, grab my keys and head for the door. Fifteen minutes later I'm cruising Sunset right outside the shuttered Whiskey when I see a figure slouched over on the curb with his head on his forearms, an overgrown blonde mohawk hanging almost to his ankles.

I pull over a few feet away and jump out of my car. "Oh my god, Bill, I am so sorry."

He looks up with squinty, red eyes, a swollen lip, and a bruised cheek. I am taken aback by a surge of guilt. Despite his outward punker appearance he is just a kid, still a boy in some ways, abandoned in a mean, dark city.

"Fuck you guys," he slurs. "After you deserted me, I had to give the bar all my money and it still wasn't enough. You guys suck. I gave everything to be in this band and you just..." His head slumps back to his forearms.

"Damn Bill, you're right. I suck." I gently put an arm under his shoulder, lift him to his feet and half-carry him to the car, all the while keeping an eye out for any black-and-white units that might roll by. This is not the first time a dude in a bathrobe has attempted to stuff a drunken kid into his car on Sunset Blvd at 3 a.m., but I would rather not have to explain the situation to the boys down at Vice.

Driving home, as Bill lies crumpled in the backseat, I wallow in self-condemnation. I ran up a massive bar tab, stuck it on a broke friend celebrating his birthday, then abandoned him to the mercy of psychopathic bouncers without so much as a "see ya later." Bill deserved better.

In the short, intense time that I had known him, we had spent almost every day together, practicing and plotting, until he became my defacto second little brother.

Though I knew he was passed-out I spoke aloud, as much for my benefit as his: "Believe me, brother, this shit will never, ever happen again."

Having procured Bill's documentation for legal debauchery, we booked our first gig at a hole called Madame Wong's West, which rose to fame 10 years earlier showcasing previously unbookable punk bands. The Knack, The Police, The Motels, Fishbone, The

Go-Go's, X, The Alley Cats, The Bangs, Oingo Boingo, Naughty Sweeties, Los Illegals, Candy, Guns N' Roses, Black Flag, No Mercy, Beowülf, Fear, Bad Actor, Red Hot Chili Peppers, The Twisters, and The Ramones had all graced that rickety stage, and now it was our turn. But Madame Wong's wasn't everything she used to be, and she didn't start out as much in the first place. The PA was blown, the lighting rig burnt out, the microphones caked with rust from the saliva of yesteryear's forgotten punk screamers.

But it was a gig, and you have to start somewhere. So, the first step on our strange, beautiful odyssey took place on a Tuesday night at 12:30 a.m. in a washed-up club in an area of town where people keep one hand on their wallet.

And it was just us.

To be fair, our friend, Eric, showed up. He was as supportive as possible, purchasing the mandatory one drink minimum, and then going above and beyond until his little, sticky table was covered in empties. He was also kind enough to supply a running commentary, providing helpful council between songs like, "You should try to be more like the Grateful Dead."

We practiced, played, and went about our daily existence in the low rent side of Hollywood, right in the epicenter of the dream/reality splatter zone. We rehearsed five nights a week without fail, crammed into a tiny closet-like practice studio in a sprawling, three-story warehouse containing 200 such closets, each with its own band beating their own dreams against reality's wall. No excuse took precedence over rehearsal. Girls, illness, car wreck, death—too bad, see you at the studio. Any heretical activity that broke the sacred rite of nightly jamming triggered an immediate "Family Home Evening," a highly unpleasant group therapy session in which your "commitment to the project" was questioned, probed, and prodded until you begged for forgiveness. An unwavering myopic focus was essential because the competition was unimaginable.

We wrote obsessively, and when we finally started playing gigs, we listened. The audience gave subtle cues telling us when we were making a connection—when the band and the crowd became a single clan, when we all reached an understanding. We built on that experience until The Uninvited shows became an "event," a happening, something bigger than the sum total of the audience, the band, and all that alcohol.

In 1995, *Rolling Stone* magazine estimated that there were well over 10,000 bands in Los Angeles. On any given night 9,999 of those bands were playing for crowds consisting entirely of a waitress and a bartender. But if you were going to see The Uninvited at 14 Below in Santa Monica, you knew to come early because a line of people would wrap around the block long after downbeat, just hoping that someone would be pulled out on a stretcher making room for one more.

The mid-1990's was still the era of the fabled "Record Deal." Music came on small aluminum discs called "CDs" with a label on one side and a rainbow on the other. A pot of gold waited at the end of that rainbow and every musician in LA would have happily sold their mom into a Turkish prostitution ring for a chance at that pot. CDs were sold in record stores, radio stations created the hits, and the entire racket was meticulously controlled by a handful of corporate media giants called "Major Labels." A Major Label deal was the music career equivalent of Valhalla, a key to the Emerald City.

Strangely, The Uninvited had major label attention starting with only our third show, but our diverse sound was impossible to categorize, and that sent marketing departments reaching for the rejection letter. In LA, the last whiff of pop metal's rotting corpse was all but gone as the dark angst-ridden sound of Seattle cast a shadow over Hollywood Blvd.

The Uninvited, however, did not fit into the Seattle's mad-at-my-dad sound, nor were we any part of the previous decade's celebration of hairspray and androgyny. We had cultivated our own sound—a melodic, jangly approach backed with 500 watts of tube-driven distortion. Powered by JT's Marshal stack on one side, my Mesa Boogie Mark IV on the other, and Bill and Bruce's gut-punching rhythm in the middle, we courted, coaxed, caressed, bashed, fondled, and battered the audience into love. A&R guys, the label's talent scouts, cluttered our guest list at almost every show, but the answer was always the same: "I wouldn't know what to do with you guys."

Due to our "unmarketability" we took the DIY road turning out CDs on our own to sell at shows and push to whatever music industry dweeb might look our way. Today, of course, "do it yourself" is the music business norm, but in the 90's, recording and pressing your own CDs was a complicated, and most of all, expensive undertaking. We borrowed from parents; we borrowed from girlfriends; we organized self-promoting "fundraisers" to beg money from fans. At one particularly low point we became so desperate for cash we got jobs. Real jobs. Where you work and stuff ... Yeah, it got that bad.

The chronic lack of funding meant that all studio time was booked "after hours," the discounted time that no one else wanted from midnight to six in the morning. Ironically, those dark vampire hours mixed with caffeine, cigarettes, sleep deprivation, and our lucky lava lamp produced a raspy raw edge that I don't think would exist had we recorded during the day.

But even more important to our sound in those recordings was the eclectic input of our producer and good friend, Jim Wirt. Jim was the owner, engineer, producer, coffee procurement expert, and musical guru at 4th Street Recording in Santa Monica, CA, where six out of seven of our independent releases were recorded.

Though a child of the mid-west, Jim's physical appearance was so stereotypical surfer he made Spicoli from "Fast Times at

Ridgemont High" look like Mitt Romney. He possessed a mountain of blond curly hair that seemed to have a personality of its own. When cutting a track, you could judge the quality of your performance by the amount of sway you induced in that mane. A little ripple meant you were doing alright, but when Jim got that mass of hair going with some inspired headbanging, you knew you were handing in a stellar performance.

On our first ever session at 4th Street I brought in the most expensive toy I owned; a rackmount distortion unit designed by Tom Sholz of *Boston* called "The Rockman." Digital technology was uber-cutting-edge at the time, and I thought I was pretty *Star Trek* with my beam-me-up-scotty rig.

Jim was less enthusiastic. He looked at my rig, looked at me, looked back at my rig, then rolled it out of the booth shaking his head. In its place he rolled in a Marshal half-stack topped with a tube-driven JCM 800, altering the course of my life.

"This is what Jimi Hendrix used," said Jim. "That shit you brought in is what Depeche Mode uses to sound like they're playing through a telephone."

The difference was stupefying. From that day forward no guitar output of mine ever passed through a transistor again.

Unlike the pristine digital cleanliness of today's recording studios, 4th Street Recording was a museum-like storehouse of archaic analog technology. In the vocal booth we sang into a massive cylindrical object that looked like something B-17s dropped on Germany in World War II. And Frankenstein's lab had nothing on Jim's control room. We played in the dark, with the light of a hundred VU meters casting shadows of Jim's throbbing hair. The tape reels spun, the lava lamp globbed, countless vacuum tubes glowed inside of steel boxes whose purpose was a complete mystery, and slowly the music took shape.

As the sun came up over Santa Monica, we would stumble out of the studio doors, shielding our eyes against the bright light reflecting off the ocean at the end of the block. Exhausted, wracked by Parkinson's-like caffeine shakes, we clutched in our hands a cassette, the precious result of a million hours of practice, blistered fingers, bleeding vocal cords, and our very last dime. It held a new song, born into a new day, as full of potential as the morning that surrounded us.

Song after song followed.

Songs became CDs and every year for five years we released a new one into the wild. We sold the CDs at our shows, and with each release our popularity grew. Yet somehow, record company love continued to elude us. They teased and fondled and promised while dangling small bits of stardom at the end of a string, but in the end the answer was always the same: "maybe"— the cruel version of "no." Thus, after six years of music industry blue balls, we planted a big kiss on the City of Los Angeles and said goodbye.

Everyone quit their day jobs. We pooled our tiny fortunes, bought a van, threw our shit in the back, and hit the road. If the labels weren't going to make us rock stars, then we would just pretend. We booked our own shows up and down the coast of California and moved our base of operations to the San Francisco Bay Area.

Strangely, we didn't fit in San Francisco either. At the time every band in SF had a conga player. Not some bands, not most bands, *every band*. Also, every band had a white guy sporting a multi-colored Rastafarian hat where they supposedly stored some vast conglomeration of whiteboy dreadlocks. I am not passing any judgments but invariably the head gear smelled like dead cat.

We knew that radio was important, but we had no way in. A small handful of Media Overlords like Clear Channel owned almost every commercial radio station in California. The Clear Channel guys played golf with the Major Label guys who in turn provided BMWs, hand jobs, cocaine, and God knows what else in exchange for airtime for their artists. Technically, the practice of "payola" was illegal but both parties had plenty of accountants and lawyers to smooth over the rough edges. Obviously, BMWs and cocaine were outside our budget, and the needle on the desperation meter was still pretty far from Hand Jobs, so we needed a different angle.

We asked around, made a few phone calls, and came up with a very short list of independent radio stations. These stations had their own in-house Program Directors and didn't get their playlists from corporate masters with new Beemers and powdered mustaches.

True to our name we showed up at these stations uninvited whenever we were in town for a gig. The nice intern at the reception desk would smile as she took our CD and then promptly toss it in the waste basket before the door closed on our backs. But we could be irritatingly persistent bastards, showing up over and over again. Between free tickets to the show, JT's eerie people skills, and occasional downright begging, we managed to slip a CD or two through the post-adolescent gatekeepers. After two months of this process we got word that KMBY in Monterey had added our song, "Too High for the Supermarket," making us one of the only unsigned bands in California with commercial radio play.

Just in case you never heard that ditty (which would put you in company with several billion people), "Too High for the Supermarket" is not your typical 1990's angst-ridden treatise on disenfranchised Gen X despondency. It is literally about being too stoned to manage oneself in a brightly lit shopping environment. Strangely, "Too High" was one of the least "crafted" songs The Uninvited ever put on an album. JT literally wrote the tune the night before a gig to keep our set fresh, and we just put it together backstage as a joke. That night, the audience's enthusiasm was overwhelming, and the song soon became a mainstay of the set.

Within two weeks listener requests drove "Too High" to number one at the station, an unheard-of event for a band without major label backing. On a particularly auspicious Monday, Rich Berlin, the station's Program Director and top DJ, gave us a call.

"Hey guys, I just spoke to Kim Stevens at Atlantic Records in New York. He was asking me how Matchbox 20 was doing, and I told him they were getting their assess handed to them by The Uninvited.

"Of course he said he never heard of you and I told him these exact words: 'Do you have a working pen? If you do than you better grab it, get out here ASAP, and ink a deal with these guys. They're number one at the station, they don't have a deal, and Capitol Records is sniffing around.'

"He told me to tell you guys that he's getting on plane tonight to come see your show in Santa Monica tomorrow." We told Rich he was the greatest human being to ever walk the Earth and we would gladly bear his children if it weren't biologically impossible.

That night we celebrated by splurging on a room at Motel 6. No crashing on friends' floors, no sleeping in the van. Sure, we had plenty of similar opportunities dry up and blow away, but something smelled different, and that was reason enough to get the party started on the credit card. Not only did we get a room, we upgraded the evening's culinary outing from McDonald's to Denny's.

Lying in an actual bed that night, savoring the feel of sanitized sheets and the not unwelcome burping of chicken fried steak, my head spun around the fact that everything we worked for over the last six years might fall into place tomorrow night. But even as I indulged myself in unbridled rock star fantasies, another thought simmered quietly below the surface:

Mia would be there too.

The Vault of Impossibility

"Eve
I think I'll have a
Bite of that apple"
- Shed My Skin, The Uninvited

Five years earlier at our third show, Mia's crushing beauty entered my life at the Central, a dark yet wondrous hole on Sunset Boulevard that would later be completely gutted to rise again as the creme de la hip Viper Room.

The Central was a starting point—square one on the Monopoly board to stardom. No club in LA would book a band fresh from the garage, but the Central wasn't picky. In its tiny confines 30 people was a packed house, so each of the five bands they booked nightly need only bring a couple of people each, whether they be parents or friends who owned them a favor. But popular bands shied away from the club. Not only did the sound system suck, a 4x4 vertical beam dominated the front of the stage, dinged, and chipped over the years where foreheads, guitars, and kneecaps met its unyielding surface.

Mia was only 20 at the time, and I was helping our good friend, Sam, sneak her into the 21-and-over bar. As I pushed the stage door open, she passed through with a small group of friends, but I didn't see any of them.

The world blurred around Mia. She had her own depth of field, making everything in her vicinity gauzy and inconsequential. Mia herself, however, stood out in sharp focus with a light that seemed to emanate from within her skin. She was small and slim, reminiscent of a well- crafted guitar: long neck with a perfectly curved body. She wore her hair long, much longer than the current style, cascading down her back in straight strands and ending in a butt that can only be described as a tiny gift from God to every passerby.

Sam briefly introduced us, and I uttered some incoherent drivel mercifully lost to the mists of time. She replied with her ever-present smile and a brief hug that conveyed a sense of lightness. I was in love with her the moment she passed through that door. But so was everyone else in the room. So was everyone else in the whole damn world. Who would not be totally, face down, hopelessly throwing-up-drunk-on-love for this girl?

I watched transfixed as she made her way to the bar, fake ID in hand. Sam laughed, loud and hard.

"Dude, forget it."

"Sorry," I said, shaking off the spell. "Is she with you?"

Sam laughed even harder. "Can you see me right now? Am I standing right in front of you? Have you met my pudgy gut?" He pointed down at his stomach. "Have you seen my rapidly expanding bald spot?" He pointed to his head. "Mia has yet to discover the inner awesomeness of Black Daddy Mac."

Sam was Iranian with very dark skin and thus fancied himself "a brother who sympathizes with the plight of the black man." He doled out nicknames to everyone he met and had assigned himself the moniker "Black Daddy Mac."

"We're just friends," he said. "She's totally cool, and we just hang out. Besides, she has a boyfriend."

"Boyfriends come and go," I posed.

"Yeah, well, I don't think she would consider your application. She dumped Jason Bateman a few years back—yeah, *that* Jason Bateman, and her current boyfriend is also rich, bought her a Jet Ski, lets her drive his Corvette." He paused. "Now let's see, you make what, zero dollars a week? And you drive a Chevy LUV from the 1800's that's barely the next model up from a covered wagon? And how about those clothes ... Do you own anything that doesn't have a hole in it? Sorry kid, I just don't see it."

"Yeah, well, thanks for the pep talk." I sighed. "But rich guys in this town can be pretty douchey..."

"Sorry," said Sam with a shake of his head, "he's actually pretty cool."

Well, that did it. Inside my heart I took the newly ignited torch and shoved it into a bucket of cold reality. A girl like her was simply not going to fall for a guy like me. Try as I might, however, a tiny portion of that torch just wouldn't go out, so I locked it away in the Vault of Impossibility right between Steve McQueen's 1967 Ferrari GTB and the Corrective Time Machine For Bad Decisions.

Eventually, we graduated from The Central and moved into bigger rooms—Club Lingerie, Nomads, The Palomino, Fair City, The Troubadour, and yes, even The Whiskey A-Go-Go.

But no matter where we went, Mia rarely missed a show. She bought our t-shirts and every CD we recorded. Through mysterious means she even managed to procure copies of unreleased demo tapes. At our gigs she invariably worked her way to the front where she would sway with her eyes closed and her head titled back, singing aloud lyrics I wrote. What did they mean to her? When a song is performed it no longer belongs to the band. It's surrendered as an offering. These songs belonged to her. They were the only things I could give her, and they were the only things she wanted from me.

Over the years, girlfriends came and went, but I always noted when She was in the room. Occasionally smoke alarms would go off in the Vault of Impossibility but that didn't matter. Safely sealed in the Vault, no desire could endanger my tranquility.

As we crawl down Wilshire Blvd. heading for the Santa Monica gig, I sit with my back against JT's Marshal half-stack, the raised iconic white logo leaving the word "Marsh" painfully imprinted into my right kidney. We have not yet installed the passenger seats into our shiny new Ford Econoline cargo van, so two out of the four of us slide around in the back with the gear, bracing feet and backs against road cases to keep from getting squished. Casters roll over toes, fingers smash between heavy sliding amplifiers.

Only 1500 miles left on this leg of the tour.

Our van is the most stripped down, no options accessory-free version made in America. If the Spartans drove to battle, they would pile into a van just like this one. Essentially, it's an engine and two seats wrapped in a steel box. When driving through the snow a mere millimeter of metal separates us from the elements and considering that there are only two heat vents on the dashboard, condensation icicles form on the ceiling in the last half of the vehicle. In the desert, since there is no air conditioning and only two windows that open, it becomes a rolling sweat lodge where Hopi inspired hallucinations are occasionally interrupted by the screams of a bandmate unfortunate enough to lean against the searing hot metal of the interior.

But despite a certain lack of amenities, the van is still our home. We sleep, eat, practice, argue, laugh, and write songs within its tiny confines. It's our house, our armor, our escape pod and we take it with us everywhere we go. Just as Han Solo loved the Millennium Falcon, we love our van.

I settle in among sharp corners and rivets of the road cases and let my thoughts wonder to tonight's gig. Our "big break" had been scheduled by the Universe countless times before, but Lady Luck, being the heartless bitch-goddess she is, always stood us up. This gig could easily end in yet another bout of Crushing Self-Doubt and Agonizing Reappraisal. But somehow, tonight felt different. The atmosphere had a certain electricity. Besides, Rich Berlin promised that Atlantic Records was flying in. Maybe this was more than just an excuse to pump-up expense accounts.

But record company string-pullers would not be the only ones at the show tonight. Out in that audience of thousands would be another person of note, happily unaffiliated with anything like the music business. I ask Tony to pass back the guest list and give it a quick scan. Mia's name was still at the top of the list, with *no* plus one. She would be, quite unimaginably, by herself.

From a tangible standpoint, not much had changed for me in the years since we first met at The Central. No money filled my pockets, holes still ventilated my jeans. The only real difference between now and then was *potential*. The heady aroma of possibility hung in the air, and that alone was enough to bolster my confidence to perilous heights.

The thought tugs lightly at the corners of my mouth as the white lines of Wilshire Blvd. inch slowly past the driver side window. The boredom induced by the traffic lulls the entire band until Bill breaks the silence: "Do you guys like sweet potatoes?"

There is a general mumble in the affirmative.

"Then why do we only have them once a year? I mean, if you miss Thanksgiving at Mom's house, then you're screwed for two years ... no sweet potatoes ... two years... "

We all ponder the statement, giving it its due consideration, and a small controversy arises out of the age-old "marshmallows on top, no marshmallows on top" debate, polarizing the group. As the two factions attempt to sway the other side with arguments like "marshmallows suck" and "marshmallows rule," we all notice a strange man standing conspicuously on the corner, though the flow of conversation does not stop.

The man is facing the street. He has his head tilted back, his eyes closed and his right hand down the front of his very baggy pants. There is a flurry of activity in his jeans, and it is obvious to all that he is vigorously manhandling his redneck friend.

"Canned sweet potatoes are okay, but I prefer when they're baked whole," says Bruce.

For another two blocks the mundane topic turns to the relative merits of mashed vs. chunky, then dies a slow, stupid death. An empty silence fills the van. Not an awkward silence, but the kind of silence that's borne out of the death of a stupid topic.

Finally, JT breaks through the dullness: "Did you guys notice that dude back there was spankin'?"

Another general mumble in the affirmative.

"Well, isn't that kinda weird? I mean, wouldn't that type of behavior prompt some kind of comment in Middle America? What does it say about us when the sight of a wacko doin' the one-handed pole dance on a street corner is not unusual enough to break-up a conversation about yams? I think our years in Los Angeles have left us dangerously desensitized..."

"...maybe if he was on fire..." said Bruce.

"I would've definitely said something if he was on fire," added Bill.

"Yeah, a guy on fire high-fiving Mr. Johnson would qualify as unusual," agreed JT.

Finally, the ketchup-like slow motion journey down Wilshire Blvd. ends in the parking lot of the Santa Monica Pier. The doors flop open allowing gear and bandmates to spill out all over the pavement. I stretch luxuriously under the warm August sun, rub my sore kidney and survey the situation.

A massive stage and lighting rig faces a dazzling blue Pacific, while the slightest of ocean breezes ripples through my long, ratty hair. In my mind's eye I picture the crowd packed all the way back to the furthest reaches of the pier, like a thousand Jesuses standing on the ocean. I smile inwardly at the potential, contemplating the Industry Big Whigs, the crowd, the show, and for a moment, I eye the lock on the Vault of Impossibility.

"Good evening ladies and gentlemen! Welcome to the Santa Monica Free Concert Series! Please put your hands together for, THE UNINVITED!!!"

JT spins on his heel and pounds out the distorted introduction to "What God Said." I sense a ripple of excitement flow through the crowd, but I'm waiting, slightly crouched, for the end of the 4th bar when Bill, Bruce, and I all come in at exactly the same moment like the charges on a building demolition.

Wait ... for ...it...

I jump into the air and come down with a gigantic "A" chord. God bless that tube-driven pre-amp. At the very same moment Bill thunders in a full octave lower and Bruce violently smashes two crash cymbals and stomps his kick pedal.

BAM!

Ten 24-inch sub-woofers rattle the foundations of the entire pier.

The high intensity intro settles down into the deep ska groove of the verse, and JT looks over at me with just the slightest nod, indicating that he wants to keep this groove going a little longer than the standard arrangement. That's fine with me.

He saunters up to the mic and pauses to scan the mass of bobbing heads. "You know what?" he announces. "I'm feeling some love tonight..."

A small cheer rises from the bobbing heads.

"...and the nice thing about it is it's got kind of an inappropriate edge to it..."

A little larger cheer.

"...kinda like we're at the office water cooler, and we don't really know each other very well, but I just gave you a little smack on the ass." JT punctuates the last line with a swipe of his hand, and the crowd answers enthusiastically. "So now we have this kinda awkward tension ... What are we gonna do? Where is this going to lead?" JT looks left to Bill, then right to me, and turns back to the mic. "Well, let's find out!" he shouts.

We bring the grove up to full throttle, JT busts into the first verse and the crowd's energy goes up five notches. We haven't even gotten to the first chorus of the first song, and yet I calculate we have about 1000 new fans. I smile and shake my head.

I wasn't even looking for her, but she stood out anyway in her usual hi-def resolution. Dancing subtly on Bill's side of the stage, she somehow wedged her petite frame through to the front row. I wandered over, mindlessly soloing, allowing my fingers to roam the fretboard on auto-pilot while my brain occupied itself with her movement.

Her dancing inspired my playing, and at that moment she raised her head and looked straight into my eyes. Normally under these circumstances I avert my gaze, *no, no, I'm not checking out your smoking hot body. Nope. I'm just rippin' this solo over here. I don't know you even exist...* But this time I held her stare.

A smile.

I returned her shy Mona Lisa with a gigantic golly-gee-shit-eating grin. Mr. Smooth in da house. She beamed, and the show was suddenly the biggest success of the tour. Who gives a flying rat's ass about Atlantic Records, I have irrefutable proof that Mia knows I occupy the same planet.

The show wraps up to explosive applause, but not before we perform the irritating ritual wherein the band pretends to leave the stage while the crowd obediently yells for more, then we pretend to reluctantly acquiesce and perform the obligatory encore. I can't count the number of times I was in the audience for this farcical display of forced adulation. If a band wants its ego stroked, then I want dinner and movie first.

Back stage I happily greet Keith from The Young Dubliners as they prepare for their set. In my peripheral vision I catch a glimpse of Mia, backstage pass in hand, talking to Sam.

We live at Sam's condo whenever we're in LA. Over the course of the next week we will eat all that's left of his food, use all his hot water, run up all his utility bills, leave drool puddles in his carpet, scatter our crap all over the place, and then leave it all there while we head off to sound check for our various LA gigs. Having us over is a little like opening a small portal to Hell in your living room.

Sam, needless to say, holds Saintly Status in the eyes of the band.

As Mia and Sam chat, I step up as casually as I can muster. They both turn to politely compliment the show, and though I am truly grateful and touched, I am also vigorously trying to generate enough psychic power to tell Sam to take a freakin' hike. Fortunately, Sam is well aware of the situation and quickly vanishes with a grin. The Cheshire Iranian.

Here goes.

"So. How's it goin'?" A solid, tried and true opener, though somewhat generic.

"It's going great," she says, "I am excited about life right now! For one, I broke up with Darren..."

Holy chocolate coated Jesus!

"...and two, I have decided to move back to Maui..."

Wait, what? WHAT?

"...I just can't handle LA anymore so I'm moving back home. I'm going to open a club and have live music by national acts. It's something that Maui really needs."

"Wow, that is so awesome!" I say, struggling to hide the fact that this is the exact antithesis of awesome.

"I have the site picked out, a business plan drawn up, and a couple of investors ready to commit."

"Wow, that is ... really ... awesome." How is it possible to be completely crushed and yet totally impressed at the same time?

She continued enthusiastically but the subtext of every sentence was the same: *I'll be 5000 miles away in a tropical paradise pursuing my dreams and never seeing or thinking of you again, not that I ever did in the first place.*

"So I have a question," she says, breaking my compulsion to go jump off the end of this pier. "How do artist and booking agent agreements work, and how do club owners build relationships with agents? And who are the good ones anyway?"

"Well, I would be happy to share with you everything I know

about chumming the shark infested waters of the Music Business. Maybe we could have dinner tomorrow night?" I heard the words come out of my mouth like I was listening to someone else's conversation. What the hell happened to preprocessing? Did my brain really authorize that sentence?

"That would be great!" she says without hesitation.

Too fast. What did that mean? Is she really excited about plumbing the depths of my brain for the tedious minutia of artist-booker relationships, or is it inarguable evidence that she wants to have my babies and live together for all eternity? Or am I a freakin' idiot who should stop micro-analyzing every syllable that falls out of this beautiful girl's mouth?

Bingo. My first rational thought of the evening.

I take a deep breath of clean sea air and summon the Inner Buddha. He settles his substantial girth into a yellow vinyl beanbag chair, summons me over, and punches me in the face. Reeling inwardly, I begin to recover until her words flow through me without dissection. Before I recognize it, a conversation is born. She is unnervingly genuine—no coyness, no flirting, no shyness, yet quick to laugh and always smiling.

She is just beginning to share with me her passion for yoga as well as music when my field of view is suddenly dominated by a blurry business card thrust into my face. I crane my neck back in an attempt to read the words when my brother says, "DUDE. KIM STEVENS, ATLANTIC RECORDS."

"No shit?" I say examining the card. "Did he like the show?"

"He blew so much smoke up my ass I think I'm addicted to cigarettes. He's talkin' to Braveheart right now. Said that Tori Amos is starting a new imprint on Atlantic and he thinks she'll want us to be the first act."

"Tori Amos? The standard-bearer of the feminist rock movement wants The Uninvited to be her first act? I'm not sure we have the estrogen levels to pull that off."

"Oh come on, we're a bunch of pussies. It's a perfect match."

I glace over at Mia whose eyes are glowing with excitement. "Wow guys, that is fantastic! If there's any band on the planet that deserves a break it's you."

"Thanks Mia," says JT, "And may I say you look particularly hot tonight?" A slight pang of envy plays through my psyche. How can he just drop a line like that and not sound like a complete asshole? JT, however, reads the current scene like a billboard. "But not as hot as my brother of course. I'm getting a heat rash just standing this close to him. Now if you'll excuse me those rat-bastards in the Young Dubs are hoggin all the Cheese Whiz on the deli tray."

Mia and I finish up the evening listening to The Dubs out on the pier, our bodies pressed together by the tightly packed crowd. I pull her in close, under the guise of making more room, and we sway and sing to the band's high-octane jig-rock. At the end of the night the lights go down, but the band milks the crowd for an encore—I love them for it.

The next night I meet her at a trendy billiards place in Santa Monica, frequented by guys in khakis and polo shirts. I'm happy with her choice as I have shot a lot of pool in bars up and down the West Coast. After all, there's not a lot to do between sound check and downbeat. The clientele here, however, is a little disconcerting. The pool halls we frequent have fewer MBA's and a lot more guys with leather vests and bugs in their teeth. As I greet her inside, I make a mental note to take it easy. Putting on a pool shark routine will do nothing to elevate my status.

Mia, however, has no such qualms. She proceeds to hand me an emasculating string of defeats, dancing lightly around the table sinking every shot with casual mastery all the while managing to be hot and delightful. I lean on my unused cue, answering her music business questions between exclamations of "Nice shot …

That's amazing ... Ouch ... Wow..." while watching the balls slam into their pockets.

After four straight clean sweeps I start to rack them up again when she puts her hand on my arm. "Sorry," she says, "You haven't even taken a shot yet. I'll rack..."

"Ya know, even if I try, I think the eventual outcome is pretty much a foregone conclusion. How about I admit crushing defeat and buy you dinner?" She looks at me for a moment, considering. "I made some spaghetti this afternoon," she says, "why don't we go back to my place for dinner?"

Victory snatched from humiliating defeat.

"That sounds perfect," I say.

On the way out the door an elderly homeless man greets her with a tone of familiarity, "Good evening, Missy."

"Good evening, Casper," replies Mia reaching into her purse. Instead of money she pulls out a granola bar and hands it to him with a smile.

"Thank you kindly, Missy," he says with his own smile, missing several teeth.

"You keep granola bars in your purse for homeless people?" I ask.

She laughs. "Yeah, I know it's ridiculous. But I know most of these guys around the neighborhood. If you give them money, they blow it on alcohol. A nutrient or two won't kill 'em."

Goddamnit! Can this girl just dial back the perfection one or two notches?

Mia gives me a ride back to her place, a tiny one-bedroom bungalow in Venice beach about two blocks from the water. As she opens the front door, she is immediately set upon by her black Labrador mutt, Ashlei, who is apoplectic in her euphoria over Mia's return. Mia is no less enthusiastic. They accost each other in a love explosion—faces licked, chins nuzzled, behinds scratched, and all I can think of is how much I want to be that dog.

She strolls toward the kitchen saying, "Make yourself at home. Why don't you pick out some music? My CD's are right there by the stereo."

I step up to a shelving unit that reaches from floor to ceiling. Running my finger along the titles, I become more confused and dumbfounded with each artist. Almost every disc on these shelves also resides in my crappy little apartment. Finally my finger comes to an abrupt halt, *The Allman Brothers Live at the Fillmore East*. I wore out two vinyl copies of this very record. It was only recently released to CD and is very hard to find.

Once again, unfiltered words fall right out of my mouth,

"Oh my god Mia, will you marry me?"

I hear her laugh from the kitchen. It sounds like waves lapping on a beach of gold coins. *Easy now fella*, I tell myself. *This girl is moving to the other side of the world. You go any further down this road and you'll find yourself in a darkened room with razor blades and Nine Inch Nails playing in the background.* Yes, some people say, "Better to have loved and lost blah blah blah." Bullshit. Just ask Vincent Van Gough, but make sure you're speaking on his left.

I pull out the Allman Brothers disc, slip it the CD tray and cue up the saddest track on the record, "Stormy Monday."

Mia emerges from the kitchen with a sauce covered wooden spoon, "Nice choice," she says as Dicky Betts caresses the intro. "This is my favorite record."

Fuck it.

I reach into the Vault of Impossibility, grab the torch and pull it into the Hall of I'm Going After This Shit. It bursts into flames down to my elbow, but I don't care. Time to stop fighting against it and start fighting *for it*. Success, however, will require focus, patience, finesse and just a little bit of Bruce Logan's Infallible Female Inhibition Removal System.

Bruce, our drummer, is good looking enough, as far as guys go, but he's no Brad Pitt. He's not anyone for that matter, but somehow girls just love him. *Really love him*. Shortly before joining the band his wife threw him out after discovering he had been having sex with everyone in a ten-block radius around his house.

The episode moved him to give up both drugs and alcohol, but women remained on the list. They bought him drinks at our gigs, the glasses and beer bottles lining up behind him like trophies as he pounded his kit. A generous and sober man, Bruce would distribute these drinks to us during pauses in the set while providing attribution to each young lady who purchased the beverage.

"This one is from the blonde over there, and this one is from the sexy thing in the tube top, and this one is from her friend who will hopefully make this evening doubly nice, if you catch my drift..."

The Bruce Phenomenon was perplexing if not downright frustrating, and we demanded answers.

"What the hell?" asked Bill one day when Bruce was dropped off at practice in a limo, a tall brunette waving goodbye through the sunroof.

"It's like this," said Bruce. "Everyone knows women like to talk, right? But just letting them talk is not enough. You have to listen. You can't just look interested; you have to *be* interested. And here's the closer, the one thing that drops a thong faster than an 8-ball wrapped in Benjamins: *Ask relevant questions.* Each pertinent question is like a double dose of female Viagra because it shows that not only are you listening, you are interested in what they are saying."

So during dinner with Mia I invoke BLIFIRS, intently focusing on her flow of conversation while injecting germane queries in the appropriate pauses, but soon I realize I don't need BLIFIRS. Her life, insights and ideas are fascinating and draw me in without effort.

She tells me the story of her Italian grandfather, who despite abject poverty in Italy, managed to scrape together "Steerage Fare" in a steamship to America. With almost no access to the upper deck he didn't breathe fresh air for seven days until finally allowed topside when entering New York Harbor. His first view of America lay at the feet of the Statue of Liberty. For the next seven years he worked in a mattress factory, alone in the New World, saving his pennies until he had enough money to bring over his wife. In the prolific Catholic tradition, they cranked out six kids, the youngest of which was Mia's father. Mia herself was the sixth child of the sixth child.

Though laughingly describing herself as a "recovering Catholic," below the surface was a profound respect for the sacrifices that helped create the life she lived. She was a college educated professional, living on the beach in Southern California, because her grandfather had enough sack to step into the unknown.

"Whoa, it's 3 a.m.!" I say looking at my watch. "I should probably let you get some sleep." I then explain that Bruce won the Chez Sammy Invitational, in which each member of the band gets a shot at trying to chip a Cheese puff into Sam's mouth at two yards with a pitching wedge. The winner is awarded couch rights while the rest of us sleep on the floor.

"I'll tell you what," she says, "I can take you back to Sam's and you can sleep on his bong-water stained carpet, or you can crash here with me. BUT..."

I struggle to hold back a touchdown pose.

"...there will be no sex."

"I would take you over Sam any day, with or without sex. Even if Sam was offering sex. *Especially* if Sam was offering sex."

I wake up the next morning (morning for me, 3 p.m. for the rest of the world) in an empty futon. Mia left many hours earlier for her job at Gigantic Faceless Corporation where she is the office manager on the 23rd floor of the Ominous Building in Century City. Ashlei lies staring at me from across the room wondering what to make of the long-haired interloper hogging her side of the bed. I know one thing for certain: the gate on Mia's heart is guarded by a black lab mutt, so it's time to make friends.

I find Ashlei's leash by the door. She explodes in a frenzy of dog hysteria the moment I pick it up. "Apparently you like walks," I say as she jumps like a pogo stick in circles around me. "Excellent."

The next few hours we spend at Doggie Disneyland on the beach. I get Milk Bones, a ball to play fetch, a piece of rope for tug-of-war—anything I can think of that dogs like. I work the dog daddy angle all afternoon until we're both panting and eager to head back to the bungalow.

The phone is ringing as we walk through the door and the answering machine picks up. The volume is cranked up; I assume to screen calls.

"Hey Mia," says a masculine voice, "it's Brad. What are you doing tonight? Let's go grab a drink. Call me."

BEEP.

"Who's this ass hat?" I ask Ashlei.

The look on her face says, "The words you speak to me have no meaning, but I could really go for another dog treat."

I slip her a Milk Bone and scratch her under the chin, but visions of "Brad" haunt me as I jump in the shower. Are they dating? Are they just friends? Hmm. An unfortunate meeting with a speeding Ford Econoline Van might be in order. The phone rings again as I step from the shower.

"Hey Mia, it's Eric. What are you doing this weekend? Hit me back."

BEEP.

Godamnit.

"What the hell?" I say to Ashlei while toweling my feral hair. Her ears spring up in full attention. In Ashlei's world any words that come out of my mouth simply mean, "I'm about to give you food."

I give her another biscuit while I inspect the phone machine. "Six messages!? This thing's a fucking box of sausages!"

The phone rings again before I can complete my thought. "REALLY? *What the fucking fuck?*" I bury my face in my hands, dreading the voice of yet another dream assassin.

"Hey Beautiful, it's me. Just wondering what you're up to. Give me a call."

BEEP.

I stare at the phone machine incredulously. How is this even possible? Is there anyone in this town who's *not* going out with this girl? My right index finger draws slow circles around the "Delete" button while an inner morality debate rages. Technology is conveniently offering an easy push-button solution to this afternoon's gargantuan buzz kill, but when all the ins and outs are measured, it's a temporary reprieve at best. My hand falls back to my side as I lean in close to the machine.

"Alright you chode farming jackholes, you wanna ro-sham-bo? Fine. Look who's standing in her kitchen and look who's simpering for attention from voicemail purgatory."

"Ashlei!" I call, and less than one second later she is right there by my side. Damn. I think I love her dog too. "Okay listen," I say while getting down to her level, "any of these douche bagels come around and you chomp 'em right in the tender bits, got it?" I give her a munchie and scratch her behind the ears.

This time, I think she understands.

An hour later Mia gets home from a day of spreadsheets, pie charts, and insipid inner office memos. "Good, you're still here," she says with a smile as she comes through the door. "I was hoping you would be stranded when I left."

We meet in the middle of the room where I get a kiss—notes of just friends, but a smooth finish rich with potential for something more.

"You want to go get some dinner?" she asks. "I'm starving."

"Nothing would make me happier," I say even though I could think of a few things that *would* make me happier, but those options are not currently on the table.

"Let me go get changed," she says, but walks into the kitchen first where she stops at the message machine.

My heart-rate increases a few BPMs as I ready myself for an Awkward Moment. I think about retreating to the bathroom so she can listen to her messages in private but it's already too late. Stephen Hawkins' electronic voice announces, "You have seven new messages. First new message..."

BEEP.

"Hi Mia, it's Mike..."

BEEP.

Mike gets cut off before he can finish his sentence.

"Message deleted," says Stephen Hawkins. "Second new message."

"Hey Mia, it's Eric..."

BEEP.

"Message deleted. Third new message."

"What's up, Mia..."

BEEP.

"Message deleted. Forth new message."

And so it goes with the entire Cavalcade of Ass Tassels. Mia decapitates the last message and turns around while I sit on the couch with Ashlei's head in my lap.

"You're a popular girl," I say with a hopefully genuine smile.

She sighs and sits down next to Ashlie and me. "What's up with my dog?" she says. "Ashlei doesn't usually like guys. She's pretty protective."

"Gosh, I don't know," I say. "Maybe it's my natural bacon scent." I scratch her behind the ears (Ashlei, not Mia).

"Look," she starts, "about those guys. They are..." She pauses to consider before saying, "...children."

"First," I say, "it's none of my business and you have nothing to explain to me. Secondly, I would like to point out, in case you have not noticed, that I am a full-grown man and have the facial hair to prove it."

"Yes," she says scratching under my goatee, "you certainly are."

Though unsure why the gods were favoring me, my first date with Mia rolled happily into its third day. The celibate nature of our continued slumber party was only mildly vexing. After all, I was taking the Long-Term View.

In accordance with our new routine, Mia went off to Corporate America while Ashlei and I hit the beach before returning to the bungalow where would-be suitors continued to beg ineffectually from the white plastic box. I didn't really pay attention anymore, thanks to a growing sense of connection and a few chin bruising sessions with the Inner Buddha.

Today, however, the white box managed to grab my attention.

"Bro!" said the disembodied voice from the kitchen, "Pick up the phone! It's me JT. Pick up NOW!"

Shit. I immediately grab the receiver: "Whoa, what's up, Bro?"

"It's Braveheart. He fucked up the deal with Atlantic. The whole thing just came apart."

"What do you mean? What happened?"

"No time to explain. Just meet me at his place in one hour."

Hamish lives in Marina Del Rey, only five minutes from Venice but about two days by bus. I decide to physically run there instead. I drop the phone, say goodbye to Ashlei and fly out the door.

When I arrive JT is already in Hamish's living room with his back to our manager. The tension is so thick it blurs my vision.

"Ok, so what's going on?" I say.

"Look lads," says Hamish, "I'm telling you this is a good thing. A good thing! My phone is ringing off the hook—Geffen, Electra,

Warner Brothers—ever since Atlantic came out everyone wants a shot at the band! It's going to be a bidding war! The Uninvited is the most sought-after band on the West Coast right now."

"Okay, so what's the problem?" I say.

"The problem is," says JT, "Hamish told Kim Stevens we were looking at other offers so Atlantic took theirs off the table."

"If we have all these other offers, what difference does it make?" I say.

JT turns to Hamish, saying, "Show him your list."

Hamish mumbles as he hands it to me.

I scan the names and suddenly the problem is Agonizingly Apparent. "Jesus Hamish," I say, "these people are nothing—nothing at all! This list might as well be blank because not one person here has any juice!"

After five years of shopping demo tapes around LA you learn who the bottom feeders are.

"That's what I told him," says JT as he rounds on Hamish. "These are errand boys and interns, NOT real A&R people. These guys don't bring bands, they bring lattes. Not one of these names has signed an artist. Kim Stephens signed Matchbox 20! He signed Hootie and every single fucking Blow Fish! Atlantic Records, for fuck sake! Led Zeppelin! Ray Charles!" JT shuts his eyes and puts his palm on his forehead.

"Did you see his shoes, Hamish?"

"Wha...?" Hamish says.

"Kim Stephens' shoes. Did you see them? Those shoes cost more than you and I make in a month combined. Kim is the real deal, and he can take the band to amazing places. Those people on your list are lucky if they can sweep the office."

"Just call him back," I say, "Tell him we were kidding. Tell him anything."

Hamish glances down at the floor. "Well, he doesn't really seem to be ... ah ... taking my calls right now."

JT and I let out a long stream of breath in tandem.

Before Hamish became our manager, he was the owner of 14 Below in Santa Monica where we were the house band for about a year. Though he had no experience in the music business, he was good at counting the bar receipts on the nights that we played. Stuffing wads of cash into his floor safe, he got to thinking about what could happen on a national level.

One day he approached us about managing the band, proposing that he sell his club and represent us full-time. We had already gone through two managers by this time, MC Doug Money and Rich V. They were good people in their own way, at least I'm sure their mothers would think so, but no matter who was our "manager" the actual management of the band always fell on the band itself, making it hard to justify the 20% cut that went to a guy who wouldn't take our calls.

We thought Hamish might work out better for two reasons. First, he had a Scottish accent which sounded really cool. Later we would come to discover that a "cool accent" was not a qualification, nor even a quality, that one needed to be a manager. We were still smoothing the rough edges of our business acumen. Second, he was not as slimy as most managers we had encountered. That's not to say that he was slime-free, but more like coated with a thin film. We figured that a slight bit of truth stretching might work in our favor. Alas, lies are like juggling chain saws—everything seems under control until the fourth or fifth one.

"We gotta fix this," I say. "I have an idea. JT you come with me. Hamish you stay here and wait for a call from Kim. If any of these Bastions of Irrelevance call just take a message, don't talk to them, and try not to screw up all of our lives."

JT brings the van around and I jump in. "Ok, here's the plan," I say. "Kim wants to use Tori Amos' imprint, right? Arthur Spivak is Tori's manager, and his office is up on Wilshire Blvd. We march into Spivak's office, explain that we've had a little misunderstanding, he calls Kim on our behalf, and we all have a great laugh together at the Grammys next year."

"It's flawless," says JT, and he guns the van up Venice Blvd towards Hollywood.

With liberal use of bike lanes, sidewalks, and back streets we are able to circumvent much of LA's legendary traffic to arrive at Spivak's office just before lunch. Having decided earlier that a full frontal assault is our best chance of success, we step right up to the receptionist's ultra-contemporary glass, teak and steel desk.

"JT and Steve Taylor from The Uninvited to see Mr. Spivak," says JT in his most authoritative tone.

"Do you have an appointment?" says the brutally fashionable woman behind the desk.

"If I said yes would you check in some kind of calendar or something or would you just escort us in?"

Perplexed, I turn to JT. "Dude, that's what you've got? Where's the magic mojo? If ever there was a time to lob a JT Charm Grenade this would be it."

"Sorry man, Hamish put me off my game." He turns to the receptionist, "Can we rewind to about five minutes ago?"

In response, the receptionist picks up the phone. "JT and Steve Taylor from The Uninvited are here. They don't have an appointment." She listens for a moment and puts the phone down. "Have a seat, gentlemen, he'll be with you in a few minutes."

Honestly, I am amazed that we made it this far. In past similar circumstances this is the point when security is usually summoned.

I sit down on a chair so stylish I'm not even sure it's furniture. A copy of *Billboard Magazine* sits on a coffee table of such intimidating value no one would dare place an actual cup of coffee on its sleek surface. I pick up the magazine, and in keeping with tradition, turn straight to the HOT 100 chart for a quick envy session. My mind's eye imagines the words "The Uninvited" on the top row. I see the bold lettering. I see the bullet. I smell the ink.

Someday muthafukas, someday...

"Mr. Spivak will see you now."

JT and I look at each other like we're about to storm the beach at Normandy and stride into Spivak's meticulously appointed office. Gold and Platinum records hang on the walls from some of his other acts including Collective Soul and Prince.

Slim and serious, Mr. Spivak looks up from his desk. "How can I help you gentlemen?"

"Good morning, Mr. Spivak, thank you for seeing us," I say. "You are obviously a busy man, so we'll get right to the point. Are you aware of Kim Stephen's intentions toward The Uninvited?"

"Yes, Kim and I have discussed it in detail. He's quite a fan. But it seems you are pursuing other opportunities now."

"Well that's just it..." starts JT.

"You see, it's our manager, Hamish," I add.

"He's Scottish," JT supplies.

"Have you ever had haggis?" I ask.

"It's a Scottish culinary abomination..."

"Made from beef tripe and oatmeal..."

"Packed in a sheep's stomach..."

"And that's how he got Mad Cow disease..."

"He was foaming at the mouth when we saw him..."

"Completely unable to make rational decisions..."

"But he's better now..."

"We gave him a Tylenol..."

"Long story short, we all agreed that Atlantic is the best home for The Uninvited...."

"And we were hoping that you might convey that sentiment to Mr. Stephens...."

"Whom we truly respect and admire...."

Spivak waits a few moments to be sure the narrative is

complete. "So you want me to call Kim and put the deal back together?"

"That, sir, is an extremely intelligent and concise summary of our humble request," says JT.

"Clearly, haggis is not in any way a part of *your* diet," I add.

Spivak picks up the phone and taps away at the keys.

I am half expecting him to say, "Mrs. Peabody, please send security to my office right away," but that is not the case.

"Hey Kim, it's Arthur. I have JT and Steve from The Uninvited here in my office. Yes ... Apparently they would like to proceed with Atlantic and the deal we discussed earlier ... Yes, their manager is on board ... He was suffering from a gastro-intestinal disorder," Spivak glances up at us over the top of his glasses. "...very well. I will let them know." He hangs up the phone and leans back in his chair.

A few tense moments pass while he eyes us with an unreadable expression.

"Ok, gentlemen, looks like we're going to make a record. Business Affairs will send over a deal memo outlining the main points before the end of the day."

Adrenaline-driven enthusiastic handshakes are exchanged all around.

"Thank you, Mr. Spivak, we really appreciate your help," I say.

"I see you are playing the House of Blues on Saturday. I'll bring Tori by," says Spivak.

"That would be fantastic," I say. "We'll leave passes at will call."

Back in the van it's a flurry of high fives.

"You're the man!"

"No *you're* the man..."

"No you're the fuckin *MAN*..."

The phrase is volleyed back and forth all the way to Culver City.

Endeavoring to keep traffic laws intact, it takes almost three hours to make the drive back to Hamish's office in Marina Del Rey.

True to his word, Kim's deal memo rolls off Braveheart's fax machine a few minutes before we arrive. With the physical offer in his hand Hamish's enthusiasm for Atlantic Records has increased significantly, hovering around the ecstasy level. However, his short-term memory has completely evaporated. He manages to take full credit for the entire deal while dropping not-so-subtle hints about how much we should be thanking him.

A portion of my ego wants to bring him up-to-speed on current events, but I'm too excited to spoil the moment in a fight with the Scotsman.

Though only an outline of the actual deal, the flimsy sheets of thermal paper lend tangibility to a dream. I don't read it, I just hold it in my hand, recalling the very first time I opened my father's banjo case and ran my finger across the strings. I was in the 6th grade. The banjo was tuned to open G—I can still hear it. From that moment, every step I took was an effort to arrive here, in this office, holding these sheets of paper. My cynical side knows the dangers: *here there be dragons*. Record company contracts range from "heavily one-sided" to "merciless sodomy." But I'm not concerned about that now. The fact that these pages even exist fills me with awe.

I ask JT for a ride back to Mia's.

She is still at work when I arrive. I pull out the biggest glass I can find in the cabinet and pour myself a gin and tonic, respectful of the fact that "gin" is the first ingredient in the cocktail's name. A large red "8" blinks at me from the message machine. Eight messages? It's a new record.

I raise my glass to the white plastic box. "Here's to you, fellas. Your persistence is annoying but admirable."

Sipping my drink, I walk to the bedroom while scanning the memo's bullet points: seven albums, tour support, promotional guarantees, quarter-million dollar recording budget ... Gin slightly watered down with tonic and just a dash of lime goes spraying out my nose.

TWO HUNDRED AND FIFTY THOUSAND DOLLARS? We made our last album for $2,500! That's 100 times more! The figure is completely inconceivable. How do you spend that much money?

The full magnitude of the deal is impossible to comprehend. I struggle with the numbers for a while then take the pages and lay them out in neat rows on Mia's futon. I carefully arrange each of the pages, so they are perfectly spaced and take up the entire surface area of the bed, like a well measured tile floor. Inspecting my work, I polish off the G&T and go make myself another. Finally, I return to the bedroom, take a seat on her linen box, and wait.

Only 15 minutes pass before Mia walks in the door. She greets Ashlei and calls out, "Hey, are you still here?"

"In the bedroom," I reply.

As she walks in smiling, her attention is immediately drawn to the bed. "What's this?"

"That, baby, is the end of the rainbow."

She looks at me quizzically. "It's my record deal," I explain. "The culmination of every hour I have practiced since I was 10-years-old. Every song I have ever written, every show I have ever played, every beer bottle I have dodged, every mile I have driven in that sweat box van, every rejection letter, every crooked promoter, club owner, and manager that made me question my very existence—it's all led to these pieces of paper." I take a long pull on my drink.

"Oh my god that is FANTASTIC!" She flies into my arms and kisses me long and hard—a strong onset of excitement with lingering notes of surrender and a solid more-than-friends finish.

The kiss melts into an embrace and she glances down at the contract. "So are you studying these? Why are they laid out like that?"

"Well ... um ... I'm really glad you asked that question." I check the dipstick on my liver: half-drunk. Perfect. "You see, there is really only one thing in the world that could possibly make this day any better..."

I take another sip of bravery fuel.

"I would like you to roll around naked on my record deal."

The sentence hangs between us like a piñata as I wait for her to swing. She inclines her head slightly to the right. Interestingly, it's the exact same reaction I got earlier from Ashlei when I told her my plan. Meanwhile the bravery juice fights valiantly against the thought that this day could go from Glorious to Shit Show in the span of a single sentence.

"You want me to roll around naked on these pages?" she asks.

I look her straight in the eye and swirl my drink with my finger. "Nothing in the world would please me more."

Holding my gaze, she puts her hand against the wall, lifts her left foot, and removes a high heel shoe. She shifts her weight and repeats the move on her other shoe. The pumps are hot. Spiked heels. I consider adding a "shoes on" caveat to the original request, but this is no time for interruptions.

Still holding my gaze she reaches for a side zipper on her tight skirt, pulls it down, and shimmies the fabric down her long, bare legs. The length of her blouse reaches to about mid-thigh and she starts unbuttoning it from the top, slowly revealing a black lace bra and matching panties. She lets the blouse fall to the floor.

I swallow so hard it's audible. Her body is a work of art. All we need is a giant clam shell to make a fully live re-creation of Botticelli's *The Birth of Venus*. She turns her back to me, reaches around and deftly unfastens her bra. She holds it out to the side with one hand, pauses for effect, and lets it fall. She then hooks her thumbs into the sides of her G-string panties and pushes them down to her ankles in a smooth, gliding motion.

I know I should say something, but my tongue is completely paralyzed. She steps over to the bed and sits down. Though completely naked she shows no sign of shyness or self-consciousness. She is, quite literally, comfortable in her own skin.

"So," she says, "I just roll around, back and forth?"

"That's it. Then my life will be complete." I swirl my drink with my finger.

Smiling, she lies back on the bed and rolls to the left, then the right, then back.

"You missed a page right over there..."

She starts laughing and rolls back to the left. Her laugh is infectious, and soon we are both howling in the absurdity of the moment.

Mia rolls on to her back and lifts her arms toward me invitingly. I fall into them and within seconds my clothes have joined hers in a pile on the floor.

Our love making is fast and explosive, driven by five years of anticipation. Breathless and reeling from the release we fall back panting on the pillows.

"Stay right here, do not move a single muscle," I tell her. "We need to get on the same page...haha." I jump out of bed, pour another G&T, and bring it back to the bedroom. We sip the drinks and connect on deeper, relaxed level. First time sex is the ultimate ice breaker.

Having caught our breath we start in again.

And again.

And again.

We move the party to the living room, the kitchen, the bathroom—not a single piece of furniture is spared the anointment of our DNA. I chase her all over the house, Ashlei barking in our wake, playing naked pirates and wearing paper hats printed with figures that stretch into the millions.

The night flies past in a drunken passionate blur until finally decelerating, slowly and happily, to the futon where it began. Mia sleeps contentedly on my shoulder, but I resist the urge to close my eyes, struggling to hang on for one more moment.

I am painfully aware of the transient nature of things. Change is the only permanence the Universe offers. But for one night in my life I hold in my hand everything I have ever wanted. Tomorrow, it could all disappear—Mia, the deal, the band, everything. So I stay awake, listening to her breathe in time with the surf in the distance. Tomorrow could bring unforeseen changes, but for the rest of my life I will have this memory, and no one or nothing can ever take that away.

Hasselhoff's Omelet of Redemption

"Wanna be billionaire?
I know how to get there
Take it out to Hollywood
There's money lying everywhere"
- Mega Multi-Media Hero, The Uninvited

Los Angeles loves to tear itself down. Obsessed with freeways and convenience stores, the City of Angels is in a constant, screaming rush to bulldoze its classic landmarks and make room for more grey, homogenous stucco. The Brown Derby, The Alexandria Hotel, Bob's Big Boy, and a thousand other iconic buildings have of all fallen to the scythe of LA's insatiable lust for Slurpees and a pathological aversion of left-hand turns. Several years ago The House of Blues on Sunset Blvd. succumbed to the same fate. Though it had lost its mojo toward the end, in the late 90's there was no gig in Hollywood more coveted than a Saturday night at Dan Akroyd's signature venue.

As the last chord of the last song in LA rings out, I survey the capacity crowd one last time. Unbelievable. The first time we played The House of Blues was a Wednesday night several years ago with six other local bands. Each band brought one girlfriend, bringing the total attendance to six. Tonight, however, we were the sold-out headliner, and girlfriends were well supplemented with a bevy of hipsters, trendsetters, gawkers, and the generally curious, all coming out to assess and judge the new kids kicking up all the dust.

Looking out at the vast fashion show before me, I'm stunned. How many times had I been on the other side of this scenario? Every time the *LA Weekly* reported a label signing, from Guns 'n Roses to The Presidents of the United States of America and everything in between, we made damn sure we went to see them, hoping to deconstruct the Secret Sauce. Sometimes the outing resulted in nothing but bewilderment and frustration. How did these song-less loser hacks ever get a deal? Other times, as was the case with Guns 'n Roses, we gathered up our cranial fragments and went home to practice, write, and refine our own sound.

Tonight, however, we were on the other side of the fish tank. The House of Blues was the only venue we ever played that sported an actual curtain. I continued to stare at the packed, cheering humanity as the curtain falls until they finally disappear behind a black velvet wall. I turn to JT with a *"Holy shit did you see that"* expression and he smiles back. It only took eight years of living in LA to be the New Kids in Town.

The highly professional black t-shirted crew strides in purposefully to start breaking down the gear while the band and I wipe sweat on towels and head upstairs to the palatial backstage area. At the HOB in Hollywood "backstage" was the upper floor and featured almost as much square footage as the main venue downstairs.

Three meticulously decorated suites formed the dressing rooms, which connected to a hallway that ended in a common lounge resplendent with voodoo artwork and a beautiful teak bar. As we top the stairs, we see that the party is not about to stop just because the show is over. We may have over-extended our headliner status a tad bit by printing up our own backstage passes, which may have fallen into the hands of about 100 of our friends. On top of that, industry scenesters eager to be associated with whatever is "next" apparently called in their favors as well.

I start wedging my way through the throng, smiling and thanking friends for their congratulations or kind words, looking for someone in particular when Braveheart grabs my arm.

"Steve, m'lad, there are some people here you have to meet!" Hamish proceeds to introduce me to Mr. Vital To Your Career,

CEO of Extremely Important Entertainment, and Joe Influential, Head Writer for Mega Industry Publication. Their practiced accolades wash over me superfluously. I realize that I'm standing in bullshit up to my knees, but somehow, I am really enjoying the crap storm.

Finally, with a last "thank you you're too kind," I am able to break free of the Beautiful Powerful People and continue my search, but alas, I am cornered yet again. A small, oval faced girl stands before me with a barely perceptible smile.

"You guys are really great," she says. The girl is wearing a plain white t-shirt, blue jeans, no jewelry and no make-up. Interestingly, her complete lack of accessories makes her stand out in the dressed up, or fashionably torn up, crowd.

"Thank you very much," I say scanning the crowd over her shoulder. "Actually I am looking for someone..."

"Your songwriting and stage presence is really something special," she injects.

A note of authenticity piques my interest. "Really?" I say, "That is very nice of you to say."

"My name is Tori," she says holding out her hand.

"Hi Tori, my name is ... *Holy shit you're Tori Amos...*"

Her barely perceptible smile becomes barely more perceptible. "I really enjoyed your show. I have your latest CD, *Artificial Hip*. I'm a big fan of that album," she says.

"Seriously? That's just amazing especially coming from you because I'm a huge fan of *your* work! I mean you are just fantastic! I know a lot of your fans are female and I'm a guy and everything, but I'm still blown away by your writing and musicianship and feel I can really relate, even though I'm not a girl, maybe because I am a big fan of the vagina..."

Holy mother of god on a biscuit I just said "vagina" to Tori Amos. I have got to chill my shit out or I can just flush this whole enchilada down HOB's tastefully decorated john.

I summon the Inner Buddha. He appears before me, gazes serenely into my eyes, places a gentle, pudgy hand on my shoulder and knees me in the groin. I let out a long whooshing breath.

"Oh my god Tori I am so sorry. I don't know what the hell I'm saying. Honestly, these last few days have been a little intense for me and I'm still trying to wrap my head around it all."

"It's no problem," she says, though her features give no indication of whether or not it actually is a problem. "Can I ask you a question?" she says, dismissing the topic. "Do you believe in God?"

Unexpected.

I wonder if an imaginary Buddha with a propensity for violence meets the criteria necessary for deity status. "Define *God*," I say.

"The first track on *Artificial Hip* is a song called 'What God Said.' I can't tell if it is serious or mocking."

"JT wrote that song," I tell her. "And I won't presume to speak on his behalf. However, when it comes to our songwriting, I can say that whatever a song means to you is much more important than what it means to us."

Her barely perceptible smile becomes downright perceptible. "It's been a pleasure meeting you...?"

"Steve," I complete her sentence realizing that I never got to my name since I was too busy fucking up my side of the conversation.

We shake hands briefly and she's gone.

That is the last time any of us would ever see our enigmatic benefactor.

I stand pondering whether or not I screwed the pooch on that encounter when two arms wrap around my waste from behind. I turn around to find Mia beaming up at me.

"Hey, I was looking for you," I say, "You just missed Tori Amos."

"Really?" she says, "Did she like the show?"

"I think so," I say, "Our discussion was mostly centered around gynecology and the hypothetical existence of God. You know, the usual small talk."

"Wow," says Mia. "I'm sorry I missed *that*."

The next morning, I pack what few belongings I have at Mia's, bringing an end to our week-long first date. Tonight we play in Las Vegas, then Salt Lake, then someplace else and so on for the next month.

I can hear her in the kitchen talking on the phone: "Hi Eric, thank you so much for the invite, but I'm seeing someone..."

"Buh-bye, Eric!" I say to Ashlei while stuffing a pair of holey jeans into my backpack. Squatting down to her level I scratch under her chin. "Listen," I whisper, "I want you to sink your teeth into any male leg that steps through that door. Actually, don't do that. It's gotta be on her terms. But a little growling wouldn't hurt."

Mia appears in the doorway and leans against the frame. I scratch Ashlei under the chin, throw my backpack over my shoulder and say for the first time the words that I will repeat a thousand times in the future.

"I gotta go, but I'll be back soon."

She kisses me—subtle notes of sadness, hints of eroticism, a lasting finish of I-miss-you-already.

Four weeks later, on a sunny LA afternoon, the van rolls up to the valet desk outside of the offices of Atlantic Records and regurgitates its human contents all over the sidewalk. The previous night's celebration—details of which were power-washed away with a pressure hose of gin and tonic—has blunted our motor skills but not our enthusiasm.

Today we sign our major label record deal. Tony, the only fully functional member of the group as usual, hands the keys to the valet while listing the vehicle's mechanical idiosyncrasies. "Stomp on the emergency brake twice if it doesn't release, and sometimes you have to jiggle the key if it won't turn in the ignition, and if it up and dies completely don't call a tow truck, just call me at this number..."

Through my darkest sunglasses I survey the automotive splendor neatly arrayed in the valet parking area—Mercedes, Jaguar, Maserati, Audi—ours will be the only Ford, and its bug-splattered grill will do little to enhance the opulence of the scene. I quietly promise myself that a year from now my ride will do that lot justice.

As we walk into the reception area, dazzling beams of sunlight reflect off so many platinum albums I feel like we are entering a televangelist's chrome mega-church. The fashion model behind the desk gathers some folders and escorts us down another platinum-lined hallway to a conference room, wherein sits a table the size and shape of a small swimming pool dotted with four large stacks of paper: our contracts.

Our attorney, Jeff, has already arrived along with Hamish and Arthur Spivak, who recently became our co-manager. Earlier, Arthur told us through his representatives in the most polite and tactful language possible, that Hamish was a ham-fisted hack who never should have left his true calling of watering down drinks and throwing out drunken bums. If the band was ever going to make it, Braveheart would have to ride off into the sunset.

Reluctantly we called a "Thank You For All You Have Done" meeting, but in the end, we couldn't do it. Hamish was a pain in the ass, but his sacrifice on behalf of the band was too big to be dismissed. As a compromise we convinced Arthur to take Braveheart under his wing, which he was willing to do—for a percentage. Thus, the band's road to profitability lengthened by a few extra miles.

Jeff slides the contract over to me and pulls a pen out of his pocket. I shake my head, reach into my own pocket, and pull out a small box. I spent the whole previous day doing something I have never done in my life: pen shopping. I hit every stationary store in LA, trying to gauge the mojo of a hundred different writing implements. Fountain pens, ball points, even flamboyant ostrich plumes were examined for magical qualities—a difficult task for someone who does not believe in magic.

In the end I settled on an elegant rosewood ball point accented with Celtic designs in pewter. Its mojo content, however, remains questionable. The pen stopped working a few weeks later.

Though the contract was stuffed with dollar signs and countless digits, what trickled down through the fine print was $5000. Each member of the band had five-grand to live on until the record started paying royalties, which could be years away or maybe never. The record company was in a big hurry to get us into the studio so the album could be released in time for us to join Stone Temple Pilots on their summer tour. It was a coveted opening slot which Atlantic felt would guarantee the record's success. We would have four weeks to make the new album if the release was going to be on time.

Arthur Spivak, the new Captain of our ship, gathered up the pages with the fresh ink and looked up at us over the top of his glasses. "I hope you guys are ready for the ride of a lifetime."

We were ready for a roller coaster, but what we got was more like a stuck Ferris wheel that someone lit on fire.

When it came to state-of-the-art recording studios LA was still the Big Cheese. Most big-name producers wanted to work in those studios, but The Uninvited loved The Bay Area and damn them all if we weren't going to record our first major label album close to home. For us, LA felt kind of like a psychotic ex-girlfriend, something better left in the past.

We spoke with a number of producers who were interested in the project including Glenn Ballard, the man who produced Alanis Morissette's *Jagged Little Pill*. We were excited to meet him because, judging by airplay, "You Oughta Know" was the only song released in all of 1995.

Ballard came to see us at Billboard Live on Sunset Blvd. After the show we met him at the bar, had a drink, and performed the mutual admiration dance. One thing he mentioned over and over was how much he loved the band's name, The Uninvited.

In the end we didn't work together, but less than a year later Alanis released what would become one of her biggest hits, "Uninvited," which also garnered a shiny new Grammy. Coincidence? Probably. But I would love to think that just maybe we contributed a tiny drop of mojo.

When it came to studios the obvious choice for us was Fantasy Studios in Berkeley. The Grateful Dead, Journey, Santana, Credence Clearwater Revival, and everyone else with a guitar and a tie dye shirt had recorded at Fantasy. But the studio had an edgy side too, giving rise to the East Bay punk scene with bands like Iggy & the Stooges, Green Day, and Rancid. JT loved to point out that "East Bay" is Pig Latin for "Beast."

Standing in Studio A on that first day was a little intimidating. I do not believe that objects retain an essence of the history of events that occurred in their presence. Artifacts are just things. But a person would have to be completely soulless not to feel some magic, some echo of the music created in this studio. As a pragmatist I tend to shy away from all things religious, yet something sacred resonated in this room. The mixing console, the tape machines, even the mic stands were all relics from a time when music itself was worshiped as a catalyst to enlightenment.

Inside these very walls prophets with strings prayed to a muse whose gifts were plentiful indeed.

The great thing about being young is that you haven't yet fully experienced the inevitable bone-shattering beatdown the world eventually delivers to everyone, leaving you lying in the street feeling like a 50-year-old bag of crushed pretzel sticks.

No, at this time in my life I had the audacity to believe that my three best friends and I would *contribute*. I was absolutely sure the performances we would record in this studio would honor the legacy of the work that came before us, inspiring another generation to sing and love, or fight and fuck, and maybe even find their own enlightenment.

Or it would suck. A failure flower blooms in every field of possibilities, but we had reason for optimism.

The producer we settled on was the semi-legendary Thom Panunzio who got his start as John Lennon's engineer on his later solo work. Since that time Thom had worked with *everyone*. I'm not going to drop a lot of names here. Just think of *anyone* who recorded in the last century and rest assured that Thom, at one time or another, was twisting knobs in a studio with that particular rock star.

Not only did Thom bring in a US-standard butt-ton of studio experience, he also brought something even more valuable: stories. We spent half the recording budget just sitting around listening to Thom's adventures in Rockstar Land, and almost every one of them started with the same setup: "I was makin' this record..."

"So I was makin' this record at the Power Station in New York," he would say after a pull on his coffee, "And on my way out I get into the elevator with Mick Jagger and Peter Wolf from the J. Geils Band. Mick turns to Peter and says, "I'll give you $1000 for those shoes."

"Peter says, 'Really?'"

"And Mick says, 'Yep.'"

"So Peter pulls off his shoes and hands them to Mick who then reaches into his pocket, pulls out a bankroll, and peels off ten one-hundred dollar bills.

"Peter says, 'Thanks.' Then he walks out of the elevator in his socks.

"So I turn to Mick and I say, 'What the hell was that about?'

"Mick just says, 'Have you ever seen that guy dance? He's incredible mate, and now I've got his shoes.' And then he walks out of the elevator too."

As we recorded, we learned Thom lived in Malibu just a few yards from the beach. His next-door-neighbor was Barbra Streisand, whose mega-star lifestyle still left plenty of time to incessantly bitch at Thom about all the regular neighbor stuff—hedge trimming, trash can placement, car parking, and loud TVs. Acres of land separated their actual houses, but Thom felt like she was just on the other side of his bedroom wall.

"So I was makin' this record at A&M in Hollywood and one of the artists recording there had this beautiful French assistant. I mean she was gorgeous! Slim with long straight shinny hair. I looked forward to seeing her every day. She had this accent that just killed me, and I would go out of my way to try and run into her whenever I could."

"So we sorta became friends, chatting from time to time in the lounge, then one day she approaches me and says she can't find any cream for her boss's coffee.

"So I say, "I'll be happy to help, and come to think of it, who is your boss anyway?"

"And she says, "*Barbra Streisand!*"

"Barbra fucking Streisand. So I say, "You can tell Barbra that if she wants cream in her coffee, she can suck it out of my dick..."

But Thom's most fascinating stories were about his late boss, John Lennon, whom Thom deeply admired. After hearing a few of these stories we asked him when was the last time he had seen the former Beatle.

"I was makin' this record with John in New York at the Record Plant. We finished up a mix and John was packing up to go home when I remembered a friend of mine wanted John's autograph. Usually, I don't bother the people I work for with requests like this, but John was very cool when it came to his fans so I figured I would make an exception.

"Anyway, just before he left, I said, "Hey John would you mind signing this track sheet for a friend of mine? He's a really huge fan..."

"John took the paper and signed his name complete with that face drawing he does. I said 'thanks' and he was off. A few hours later me and Jack Douglas, the producer, are sitting in the lounge when on comes the news—John Lennon's been shot.

"We can't believe it, we're in shock, scrambling to get to a phone to find out if it's real. What a fucked up night, probably the worst in my life. No one can sleep so we're all up talking to people, all of us just trying to wrap our heads around this massive tragedy. Finally, I get back to the hotel with the sun coming up and as I'm pulling off my clothes, I find the autograph. And I think to myself, '*This is John Lennon's very last autograph.*'"

"Holy shit," says JT, "you have one of John Lennon's very last autographs?"

"Nope," says Thom. "A few days later I saw my friend and I gave it to him."

"WHY?" asks Bill. "Why didn't you keep it?"

"Because I said I would get it for my friend, and John signed it for my friend. I couldn't live with myself if I had held on to it."

And thus, Thom gained our life-long love and respect.

. . .

Having a recording budget larger than the Gross National Product of Uzbekistan is exhilarating and embarrassing all at the same time. Foremost it allowed us to buy studio time outside of the business hours of fruit bats. We had recorded in the middle of the night for so long that it felt almost decadent to face a microphone without wobbling from sleep deprivation.

Then there was the food. Whatever we wanted, whenever we wanted it. Two weeks earlier food was a luxury indulgence usually replaced by air or maybe water if there was enough money to pay the water bill. In the studio, however, you just told the receptionist you liked the filet mignon from French Laundry, and 30 minutes later it's waiting in the lounge complete with a nice cabernet selected by Thomas Keller himself.

But the ultimate lesson in rock star dinning came from Thom, our Mentor of Privilege. No matter what restaurant we chose, our producer ordered no less than four different entrées. For himself. Thom was lean and fit, so the massive caloric extravagance was mystifying, but the reason for his svelte waistline soon became clear. He took one bite from each to-go box, then left them on the table.

"Thom," I said after witnessing this ritual several times, "what gives? Isn't that a waste?"

He looks at me like I'm a yeti wearing a fez. "Are you kidding?" he says. "I don't know these restaurants. I don't live here."

"So?" I say.

"Well," he says as if he's talking to a kindergartener, "what if you order something and you don't like it?"

The band's dinner order that evening consisted of no less than 24 entrées.

Well-fed and well-rested, the band cranked out track after track despite a never ending series of interruptions from Industry Potentates demanding Thom's immediate attention. Cell phones were still a rarity at the time, so the commandments would be delivered via receptionist.

"Mr. Panunzio, there's a Mr. Impressive from Enormous Records on the phone..."

"Tell him I'll call him back," Thom would say.

These distractions would take place about 20 times a day, to the point where frustration was setting in. Every once in a while, however, the name was just too big to blow off.

"Mr. Panunzio, Bono is on the phone for you."

Bono. That's a personal pronoun that requires no qualifying prepositional phrase. On the other hand if someone were to say, "Steve is on the phone," you've narrowed down the range of possibilities to about one-third of the world's population. "Bono," however, can only mean one man.

Thom turns to me and says, "Do you mind if I take this call?"

"You tell that hipster leprechaun freak this is The Uninvited's time and he can go chill his shit out with another bowl of Lucky Charms." At least that's what I meant to say. The words that actually came out of my mouth were more like, "Wow, really? Bono? He's on the phone right now? That's so cool! Of course, man, you gotta take that call; it's freakin' Bono!"

Despite the stories, the food, and the endless interruptions, we manage to crank out the tracks in about half the time we were allotted in order to meet the deadline for the Stone Temple Pilots tour. We had five years to prepare for this album, so in all honesty we could have recorded the whole enchilada using nothing but our feet. Every record we made to this point was just a practice run for the Real Thing. In fact, only two new songs appeared on the record, "Young and Beautiful" and "Velcro Heart." The rest were from our catalog.

Strangely, our major label debut would be a greatest hits record.

Though we managed to get the label to agree to record the album in the Bay Area, they insisted that the final mix take place at A&M Studios in Hollywood. A&M had just installed brand new magic digital sorcery, but we passed on the performance enhancing fuckery in favor of good ol' fashion reality. In the end, the album would just be musicians playing and singing into microphones.

As the last mix pours over onto the quarter inch reel-to-reel, Kim Stephens strolls purposefully into the studio. Part of Kim's duties as an A&R man is ensuring that the band didn't spend a quarter-million dollars creating a musical dung heap. If he didn't like what he heard he could pull the plug right there, sending us back to a life of single entrées consisting of air. What Kim really wanted to hear, what all A&R guys want to hear, is the sound of money. Good A&R people have a freakish ability to divine what the world is going to like next year. They can hear the cash deep in the track, and they call it a hit song.

We exchange pleasantries but Kim is all business. He is not here to be our friend. He is not here as a doe-eyed fanboy. He is here to pass judgment on the commercial validity of our life's work.

As judge, jury, and executioner settles onto a sofa centered perfectly between two small, near-field monitors (speakers that best simulate how the majority of people listen to music: a crappy car stereo). He clasps his hands in his lap and bows his head as if he is going to pray. The posture induces silence. He gives the slightest nod, cueing Thom to press a single button on a mixing console studded with thousands of identical buttons, and the resonator guitar intro of the first track, "Mega Multi-Media Hero," fills the room.

While the riff kicks its circular groove, I study Kim for any hint that might expose his thoughts. His left foot taps on the backbeat... And damn, look at those shoes. They must be Italian. I imagine some Geppetto-like cobbler hand-tooling the supple leather in a back-alley shop somewhere in Florence, Italy. Did that cobbler consider the person whose foot his handiwork would encase? Could he have possibly imagined that his finely crafted loafer would one day swaddle toes that kept time to the frail dreams of four desperate musicians? Whoever created these shoes was an artist. Mr. Stephens wore artwork on his feet.

The song comes to its abrupt end on the word "hero."

Kim looks up from his penitent position and says to no one in particular, "That's a hit song. Top down on the Pacific Coast Highway, stereo blasting. Great Summer release. We'll hold that for next June."

"Cool," says JT, trying to sound confident and relaxed. But I hear the undertone of a man struggling to contain a cataclysmic victory explosion. Personally, I'm trying not to bawl like a newly crowned Miss America.

"Sounds good," I choke.

The next song up is "What God Said."

"That's the first single," declares Kim matter-of-factly.

"Bitchin," says JT.

"Fuckin-A!" says Bill.

The facade of cool crumbles to the ground. High fives fly in every direction.

JT slaps Kim on the back, saying, "Damn you have good taste in music!"

For the rest of the listening session we are on our feet, pacing, humming the tunes, trying not to disturb Kim's reverie yet crowding him expectantly after each song. He never disparaged a single track, and four tunes got the golden moniker: "That's a hit song."

We celebrated that night down the street at the legendary Rainbow Room, whose hallowed barroom floor had been thrown-up upon by every member of our label mates, Led Zeppelin. The drinks flow but we manage not to contribute any of our own gastric juices to the well anointed floorboards.

At the end of the evening, a yellow taxi drops me off at a hotel so stylishly contemporary it must have been built 10 minutes before I arrived. I fall into my luxurious king-sized bed, courtesy of Atlantic Records, and dream I had dinner with Bono.

We ordered 16 entrees, and I picked up the tab.

Every morning since our first date, I asked Mia to marry me. It had become a ritual of sorts, harkening back to my initial, unfiltered proposal blurted out five minutes after first seeing her CD collection. With the new record completed my confidence grew to irrational proportions.

"I gotta get to work," Mia says as we sprawl lethargically on the futon.

"Will you marry me?" I ask.

"Yes," she says.

"Then why are you going to work? We're on the verge of redefining pop culture over here and you want to run off and deconstruct pie charts or something. Blow it off. Let's go mansion shopping instead."

"Ha!" she says. "Don't get me wrong, I have all the faith in the world, but in the meantime, there are little things like rent and food."

"Baby, I got two-hundred bucks from last night's gig. We're covered. Let's go to the Ferrari showroom up on Wilshire."

She gives me The Eyebrow, a look more layered in indecipherable meaning than the collected works of E.E. Cummings. (I don't want to get into a lot of foreshadowing here, but The Eyebrow will eventually become such an integral part of my days with Mia that I will actually be able to *hear it* over the phone).

I laugh and make a snap decision. While up north recording the album, I had stopped by a jewelry store and dropped my record company advance on a modest diamond ring.

When I told my brother I was working on closing the deal for him on a brand new sister-in-law, his smile, though genuine, carried signs of resignation around the edges. JT was the first person in the band to take the leap into matrimony, marrying a stunning actress named Eris after graduating from USC. Eris had a porcelain complexion framed in fiery red hair, perfectly matching a fiery passion for, well, everything.

On the surface JT and Eris were a perfect match, two passionate people being passionate all the time, especially in other people's bathrooms. To JT and Eris a closed bathroom door was a double dose of Viagra sprinkled with rhino horn and wrapped in tiger scrotum. No restroom was too small, no gathering too intimate, to preclude a noisy toilet top rendezvous. Eventually, we all just got used to it.

"That's fantastic, Bro, congratulations!" JT said pulling me in for a hug.

"Thanks, Bro," I replied. I stood back and met his gaze straight on. "Are you okay with this?"

Complete, total, brutal, painful, bludgeoning honesty had been the corner stone or our relationship since we first started writing songs together. If JT had a problem with the familial expansion, he would let me know.

"Bro," he said, "I love Mia—everyone loves Mia—she's smart, kind, engaging, a total crack-up, and if I may say, disconcertingly beautiful. Among your peers, and by that, I mean me and Bill and Bruce, you are pretty much considered lucky as hell and out of your league. So of course I'm happy for you! But marriage in general, as an institution, that's..." He considers some far-off object visible only to him "...challenging," he decides. "And frustrating, and glorious, and exhausting, and life-affirming, and ... Did I mention frustrating?"

"Here's the crux of the matter," he continued. "*Can you live without her?* The answer to that question is important. In fact, it's critical. You have to know in your heart-of-hearts that you simply *cannot live* without this girl, and here's the reason why: someday, you will want *to kill her.* Really. Not kidding. And the only reason that you don't kill her is because you *cannot live* without her." He pauses again to reflect. "Did I mention frustrating?"

Though I had never given that angle any thought before, the words dropped from my lips with equal amounts conviction and surrender:

"I cannot live without her."

Lying in the futon with Mia I was impatient to get the party started. I had planned a one-knee-on-a-moonlit-beach proposal, but in order to keep her in that bed I needed a hallelujah moment to help her grasp the magnitude of the spectacularity that shined just around the corner. Besides, I really wanted to go see some Ferraris.

I reached under the bed and pulled out a small velvet box. Maybe the daily proposal had desensitized me to the real thing, but the moment that little upholstered package entered the morning light the entire Universe came to a complete stop.

Breathing paused, street sounds went silent outside the window. Without warning my bullshit confidence unexpectedly crumbled under the weight of the possibility that her response, when it really counted, would change. My eyes moved from the box to her face.

Tears gathered in the corners of her eyes, but tears of joy and tears of sadness are indistinguishable at first glance. I studied them for a moment, hoping for a clue, but realized that no answer would be forthcoming until I asked a question.

I summoned the Inner Buddha.

Nothing.

Really you fat fuck? *This* is the time you're going to abandon me?

When you look back on your life, the moments that created

"before" and "after" are perspicuous, boldly highlighted on our time maps with bright push pins and red arrows. But during the actual event, the transitional seconds that define the end of one chapter and the beginning of the next stretch to the point of infinite elasticity. I remember the pattern on the bedspread. I remember the soft feel of the sheets. I remember the weight of Ashlei's head resting on my calf.

"Mia, will you marry me?"

I open the box toward her, as though a small rock and a bit of gold will shatter any lingering doubts. Pay no heed to the fact that the decision you make at this very moment will determine your happiness or misery for the rest of your life. Just say "yes" and this shiny trinket is yours.

The tears gather in earnest until finally escaping her long eyelashes. They run unimpeded down both cheeks. I catch them with the back of my finger.

"Yes."

The problem with being a "sensitive artist type" is the "sensitive" part. In an attempt to conceal my own tears I kiss her, hard; our slippery wet faces rubbing together to hide the evidence of my lack of composure. A good deal of snot is involved, but slimy affection is the very best kind, and we revel in it. A lot. So much so that not only did she miss work, I didn't get to see a single Ferrari.

I hear the crushing news for the first time while watching *Entertainment Tonight*. Though scrutiny of celebrity flotsam is the modern equivalent of trepanning, sometimes you just can't pull your eyes off a train wreck. Regardless, the nice blonde lady, whose journalistic aspirations died breathless in Michael Jackson's iron lung, reads the teleprompter with canned gravitas:

"Scott Weiland, lead singer of the alt-rock band Stone Temple

Pilots, was arrested today and charged with possession of heroin..."

Fuck me.

Our first big arena tour starts in four weeks opening for this jackasstrophe's band. Atlantic is rushing the release of the album specifically for this tour. Everything is teed-up for success, but the swing just rebounded into a crotch shot.

A flurry of panicked phone calls elicits the requisite hand jobs —it will be fine, everything is fine, don't worry about it. But a few days later when Weiland stands before the judge the word comes down: mandatory rehab.

The tour is cancelled, the album is shelved and The Uninvited are banished to career purgatory.

In the years to come Scott Weiland will die of his addictions, leaving behind devastated children and a pissed-off ex-wife.

Mary Forsberg, the mother of his kids, will release an open letter about her ex-husband stating in part, "I won't say he can rest now, or that he's in a better place. He belongs with his children barbecuing in the backyard and waiting for a Notre Dame game to come on. We are angry and sad about this loss, but we are most devastated that he chose to give up. Let's choose to make this the first time we don't glorify this tragedy with talk of rock and roll and the demons that, by the way, don't have to come with it."

The sad truth is Weiland's story is the typical outcome of the second caveat in "Sex, drugs, and rock and roll."

For every Keith Richards there are a thousand Scott Weilands.

In our years on the road we will share the stage with hundreds of musicians, each harboring dreams and demons like everyone else. I found that substance abuse is no more prevalent among working musicians than board room jockeys, roofers, dishwashers, or any other person trying to make a living in this world.

In fact a brain swimming in vodka or a nose packed with cocaine only

makes the job harder, and almost always destroys the musician long before
success can blossom. A band might tolerate a vomit-drenched drummer for
a little while but the stuffy confines of a hot van rolling through the desert
takes all the romance out of the smell of stale urine and half-digested
Big Mac.

The tragic appeal of the "troubled artist" fades fast, quickly replaced
with a boot in the ass and a bus ticket home.

Despite the Stone Temple Pilots setback, I remained confident,
buoyed by my elevation in status from "boyfriend" to "fiancée."

Excluding my daily marriage proposal, the next morning
retains its usual routine. Mia wakes up early for work. I do my
best to explain the folly of such behavior. She rushes about the
bungalow, hurriedly trying to get ready in a state of perpetual
tardiness. I suggest that sex would help but am unable to
vocalize the exact reasoning without coffee. She gives me The
Eyebrow, I press my case with a bit of a shoulder rub, she
acquiesces, then takes a more leisurely approach in the
aftermath despite being twice as late as before. She kisses me on
the way out—yours forever with notes of Just Wait Until
Tonight.

Ashlei is also well aware of the routine. The moment Mia
leaves she is sitting at the door, staring at her leash and wagging
her tail.

"Alright girl, let's do it." I have enough mental clarity to put on
board shorts and roller blades, but that is all.

I stumble awkwardly into the morning sun, snap the leash
onto Ashlei's collar, and let her pull me to the coffee shop down
the street, blinking and rubbing my eyes. Small but strong, she's a
good musher and kindly allows me to arrive at our destination
without a single thrust of my blades.

Still blinking I roll right up to the counter. A massive

chalkboard covered with java-related concoctions adorns the entire wall behind the bar.

"Coffee. Just coffee. And a biscuit for the lady."

Energized by our sustenance, Ashlei and I begin our trip up the coastal bike path in earnest. If Los Angeles is a circus, Venice Beach is the sideshow. On the left, the Pacific Ocean glitters. On the right, the opening strains of the Boardwalk Freak Show greet the morning.

Harry Perry, sporting his iconic white turban and flowing robes, extorts tourists with a Raga Jimi Hendrix routine on roller skates, berating his victims with dissonant guitar riffs until they pay the audio ransom with a few quarters. Street vendors prop up stalls selling everything from palm readings to henna tattoos, but counterfeit sunglasses rule the boardwalk. Every 20 feet another rack of plastic five-dollar Oakleys, Ray Bans, and Ralph Laurens beckon the fashion conscious yet financially challenged. Rest assured that anyone wearing Gucci sunglasses within a 10-mile radius of Venice most likely has a headache.

Ashlei and I continue up the coast at a good clip weaving between the pedestrians and slower bladers. Up ahead a film crew has setup with reflectors and camera cranes, not an unusual site on the beach. On the edge of the bike path, a clump of people mingle around a central figure nodding heads, pointing at clipboards, and gesticulating deferentially. Ashlei and I have our groove on when, without warning, the entire clump of people shuffle blindly into the path in front of us.

Too late for braking. I let go of Ashlei's leash, aware that her nimble paws will effortlessly skirt the obstruction, while I plow into the closely packed minglers like a bowling ball. Elbows, heads, and other unforgiving body parts pummel me as my skates leave the ground. A tiny voice in my head notes that ungrounded skates are a bad thing, since gravity will require that some other part of my body take their place. Through the variances of Newtonian physics and Chaos Theory that body part turns out to be my right knee, which acts as both shock absorber and brake, leaving a three-foot skid mark of blood and skin on the cement path.

I writhe on the ground clutching my knee like an 8-year-old with a boo-boo as Ashlei licks my ear. She is the only one to come to my aid. The Clustered Obstacle People immediately spring to their feet to assist the Central Figure, whom I recognize through watering eyes as David Hasselhoff, star of the TV lifeguard drama, *Baywatch*.

Hasselhoff's first success was *Night Rider*, in which he co-starred with a talking Trans-Am. When that show faded away, his career went to the next level after enlisting an even more appealing co-star: boobs, most notably those attached to Pamala Anderson. *Baywatch* was a boob-a-palooza with scores of them all jiggling in lifesaving runs down the beach, barely contained in bright orange bathing suits. Millions of pubescent teens nationwide experienced weekly fantasies of drowning on this very stretch of coastline.

Despite their enduring appeal, boobs are not really on my mind at this moment. Searing white-hot pain has blocked all body parts from my thoughts with the exception of my knee. As the entourage shuffles Hasselhoff away with murmurs of concern I am literally left bleeding by the side of the road. *Baywatch,* already low on my list, drops another few notches. Any respect or admiration I may have harbored for David Hasselhoff's work is slipping fast, despite his quippy banter with cars and breasts.

Slowly, unsteadily, I rise up on my skates to test the knee. Though crusted with sand and blood, it works. Despite the pain, an unexpected yet delicious scent of frying bacon captures my attention. Glancing around for the source I see that craft services has setup for the shoot, dishing up top notch Hollywood vittles for the hardworking cast and crew. Ashlei smells it too. Ears up, her whole body points to the Celebrity Chuckwagon like a protein divining rod. I pull a blood-clotted sand clump from my knee.

"Ashlei, I think Hasselhoff owes us breakfast."

My brother always says, "If you look like you're rocking, you are rocking." That philosophy got us through some very unrehearsed material, but it also applies to life in general. Simply looking like you know what you're doing will get you through 90% of situations that otherwise require real qualifications. We confidently cross the sand to join the line of PA's, Grips, and Best Boys queuing up for breakfast, brought to you by NBC.

Unfortunately, despite my best air of harmless neutrality, the girl taking omelet orders gives me a second look. "I'm sorry, do you have your laminate?"

Hmm, I had assumed the universe would clear the path to breakfast considering recent injustices—must be a snafu in the Karmic Accounting Department.

"Life is not fair," Dad used to say. Why is that guy always right? It's not fair.

As I contemplate my bulletproof response to Omelet Girl a metallic glimmer flashes next to me. It's a badge. Not the plastic chrome toy badge of a rumpled security guard, but the bonafide silver sparkler that beams from the chest of LA's Finest. Many production companies use off-duty cops as security during on-location shoots.

Officer Large looms next to me, patiently holding an empty plate. I give him my best good morning smile but cannot help noticing the large baton that hangs from his belt. It has some pretty deep divots. The wood shows through where paint chips are missing. I decide that lying would only compound the day's injustices, so I turn and look the girl right in the eye.

"It's okay, I'm with the band."

The Golden Phrase. For 15 years that sentence has granted me uninhibited access while excusing countless transgressions and misdemeanors.

Without a moment's hesitation the omelet girl smiles wide and says, "Awesome! What would you like?"

About 200 yards between me and this gigantic cop ... "Oh, anything is great, just throw some bacon in there. Don't want to clog my arteries with too much vegetable matter."

Two minutes later, Hasselhoff's Omelet of Redemption graces my plate. All is forgiven. I might even briefly pause while channel surfing should I chance upon the breasts of *Baywatch*. I give a good sized omelet chunk to Ashlei and decide not to join the rest of the crew at the tables. An over-abundance of caution is rarely the cause of knee divots in police batons.

Later that night back at the bungalow I share the story with Mia, but I never get to finish the tale. Just as the words "David Fucking Hasselhoff" leave my lips, fully automatic machine gun fire erupts a few houses away. The growing gentrification of Venice Beach still hasn't pushed out the gang problem. The hood, in fact, is only one block over.

I immediately grab Mia, fall to the floor, and roll over on top of her—something I have become pretty good at lately. As we lie there listening to the shots rattle off I once again sigh at the lack of fairness. Why is it when a war zone breaks out in my neighborhood a police cruiser won't show up for 45 minutes, yet if I am partaking in even the most minor of infractions there is a cop is standing right *next* to me.

It's the last insult. Between the Celebrity Aristocracy and the nightly clatter of Glocks, I am done with LA. The band had already moved to the Bay Area and it was time to take Mia to the promised land.

Later that night, lying in bed, I convince her that it is time to go make a home of our own.

But it would have to wait.

Though the Stone Temple Pilots tour was dead and the album in limbo, we still needed to lay the groundwork for the record's eventual release. Braveheart and our booking agent, Kevin, hooked us up with the opening slot for the Violent Femmes, which starts in a week in Wisconsin.

A few days later the van rolls up, the door slides open and the horn beckons. I kiss Mia, scratch Ashlei on the head, and stroll out the door.

Pain, Patties, and Postponement

"She doesn't find
My open mind
Too reckless
And I don't care
That her whimsical stare
Leaves me helpless"
- She Moves Me, The Uninvited

It turns out that America is only 20 minutes from Los Angeles. Once you leave the coast and pass the LA County line, America's bounty reveals itself in an endless expanse of strip malls, each with a Walmart on one side and a McDonalds on the other. Mile after mile, city after city, state after state, it's the same food, the same beer, the same gas, and the same horde of plastic doo-dads manufactured in China for doo-dad starved Americans. All of this is relentlessly offered over and over again like nationwide green eggs and ham.

"I do not like them Sam I Am…"

"Excuse me?" says JT.

"Nothing." I sigh, staring out the van window as yet another set of golden arches rolls by. How is it possible that a Big Mac awaits at the end of every offramp? Do the laws of supply and demand no longer apply in Middle America? At sixty-miles-per hour, a McDonald's opportunity presents itself *every ten minutes*. Some genius sociologist must have determined that the constant suggestion, combined with the hypnotic effect of highway's dotted white line, creates an undeniable longing. You might pass up the first ten or twenty Micky-D stops, but eventually, you're gonna have some fries, bitch.

The repetitive nature of the scene out my window enhances the feeling that we are going nowhere. Without a release date for the album it feels as though the band is stuck in cold storage. If the AC worked, the metaphor would be perfect.

The cell phone rings. It's the digital sound of money leaving the band fund.

JT checks the number, gives me the "Sorry Bro" face, and thumbs the connect. "Hey Baby..."

It's his wife, Eris. I watch my brother's face as it transitions from unexpected delight to please lobotomize me.

"I don't know what you're talking about," JT says into the phone, forehead wrinkled in annoyance. "Wait, back up..."

The volume from the phone rises perceptibly. The actual words are indecipherable, but the anger is clear as the sun beaming through the windshield.

JT pulls the phone away from his ear. "Jesus Christ are you kidding me? Really? That never happened! Never happened!" His voice rises steadily with the phone volume until he is holding the brick-like handset a foot from his mouth.

"Godamnit Eris, how long have you known me? You know I would never..."

The verbal assault emanating from the phone's tiny earpiece is an unrelenting stream of vitriol without so much as a single pause to inhale.

"Eris..."

"Eris..."

"ERIS!!"

There is a pause, then he says, "YES, SHE WAS A GIRL. 50% of the population of the Earth is made up of females so I might run into one from time to time. That does not mean I have sex with them. Meeting one and fucking one are entirely TWO DIFFERENT THINGS."

JT's solid line of reasoning fails to stem the flood of acrimony. Holding the steering wheel in one hand and the squawking phone in the other, he looks over at me like a drowning man. I rifle through my conscience searching for an emotional lifeline when his face suddenly goes calm.

"Baby ... Baby, listen to me. I love you. You know there is no other girl I could possibly..."

The phone goes dead.

He puts the handset down and lets out a long breath. An awkward silence settles over the van. It's impossible to maintain a discrete distance when you are forced to sit butt cheek to butt cheek. Still, it's none of our business, so we all busy ourselves looking out windows or picking invisible lint off our shirts.

"She heard that the receptionist at KMBY really likes us," JT offers in monotone. "Thus, there can be no doubt that I'm doing reverse cowgirl with her on the broadcast desk."

"I would totally do reverse cowgirl with that girl anywhere," says Bruce.

"Shut up," says Bill, "This shit is real."

Frustration takes the form of bulging veins on the back of JT's hands. The irony is that my brother is pathologically monogamous. Night after night a buffet of carnal pleasures are laid out before him, free for the taking, but he only hungers for one dish. Furthermore, he and Eris have a young toddler which only reinforces his myopic, steadfast devotion. Eris knows all of this. But distance mixed with vodka and a splash of crying baby has a way of distorting perceptions.

JT's dustups with Eris are troublesome in several ways. First, they elicit within me a primal protection response that dates back to the playground. Though my personal "fight or flight" instinct defaults to "flight" in pretty much every scenario, messing with my brother triggers an unusual face-breaking-rib-snapping rage. All I want to do is step between my brother and trouble and get busy with a cue ball in a tube sock. But in this circumstance, all I can do is sit and quietly seethe to myself. A broken beer bottle street fight with my sister-in-law would have unpleasant consequences, both legal and personal. Plus, she would probably win. Regardless, it is a good thing she's 500 miles away.

The other problem with these digressions from marital bliss is that they suck all the charm juice right out of JT's soul, leaving him a musical automaton when we take the stage. The power chords have no power. Between song banter is reduced to arena rock clichés delivered with robotic enthusiasm.

"How you doing, Cleveland? Are you ready to rock?"

Band and audience suffer alike.

Thankfully, that is not the case when we arrive at the University of Wisconsin-Madison for our first show with The Violent Femmes. At this time, The Uninvited has no airplay in Wisconsin, no local following whatsoever. We are the archetypal Opening Band, the buffer between bong hits in the parking lot and the first song of the headliner. We are the muffled background music you hear while standing at the urinal checking your seat number, trying not to splash the guy next to you.

But judging from the lack of empty seats the student body at UW have exemplary time management skills. Bladders have been emptied, self-medications fully administered, and seats found all before show time. This is our first ever arena gig, and the old cliché *"packed to the rafters"* applies. People in the upper most rows can literally touch the ceiling. Never before have we had to crane our necks up to see the bulk of the audience.

A crew member leads us to the side-stage stairs. "Just wait here until the lights go down, then walk up to the stage. When you're all plugged in give me the high sign and we'll tear this place up, cool?"

We nod our heads like four bobble head dolls.

But when the lights finally dim, we are unprepared for the reaction. 8,000 college kids erupt like it's raining beer. My first thought is there must be some mistake. Did they not read their ticket stubs? Are we here on the wrong night? I look around half expecting to see Nirvana shoulder past us up to the stage. Slightly disoriented, we walk up the steps and plug in our instruments, certain there will be a massive sigh of disappointment when the lights come up.

JT looks around to see if everyone is ready. He gives me the half grin, indicating he came here to *work*. Any lingering emotional residue from his earlier spousal upheaval has been washed away by the screaming throng. For myself, however, the din offers no therapeutic effect. On the contrary, the volume of the crowd is directly proportional to my increasing level of self-doubt. Why are they so loud? They have no idea who we are. We could be introducing these fine people to a whole new level of suck, yet they seem to assume that something amazing is going to happen when those lights come up.

I summon the Inner Buddha.

The crowd noise fades into a slightly distorted, toy piano version of "When the Saints Go Marching In." It's an ice-cream truck. Childhood memories fill my frontal cortex, rich with the sugary artificial flavors of Popsicles, Drumsticks, and Pushups, their melting goodness running in gooey rivulets down my forearm. The van stops right in front of me. A menu of frozen delights beckons next to a sliding glass window. Inside the truck I see the Buddha sitting in lotus position, his face the very essence of serenity.

I step up to the window. "I'll have a..." But before I can finish my order the van lurches forward running over my foot. I hear the muffled crunch of bones snapping through my Converse sneakers...

The lights come up, but I hear nothing. My full attention is captured by the flight of a single shoe sailing toward us through a smoke-filled spotlight. My subconscious does a quick calculation and maps the trajectory straight to Bill's head. I yell to warn him knowing full well he can't hear me, but it's unnecessary. He sees it. Inches before impact Bill tilts his head 45 degrees and the shoe sails past his right ear bouncing harmlessly on the stage.

Someone is going home tonight with one shoe—that's going to be uncomfortable.

The crowd explodes in my ears. I read the "One two three four!" on JT's lips, and we rip into "What God Said."

The crowd shows no sign of disappointment.

In the years to come I will learn that not all audiences are jaded with pre-conceived notions of hip, but at this moment I embrace Wisconsin with a loving heart. Song after song we do our thing whipping the audience into a frothy meringue until we are all just one big sweaty mess by the end of our set. An unplanned encore ensues before we retreat side stage baffled but exalting in our reception. We mill about backstage waiting like everyone else for the Violent Femmes.

The headliner takes the stage ripping into a familiar repertoire of hits, inciting more hysteria from the collegiate masses. I'm surprised by the meaty auditory attack generated by three acoustic instruments, reinforcing my belief that attitude and passion, not virtuosity, form the scaffolding of great rock 'n roll.

Off stage, however, the Femmes are reclusive and inaccessible. Not only do we have separate dressing rooms, they retreat to the busses the moment the last note fades. For the next three weeks it's the same strange routine. College kids go crazy, we do our best to work the crowd to just short of a riot, then the Femmes punk up the room with acoustic instruments before evaporating into the night. I never get a chance to thank them for our first taste of Arena Rock Mayhem.

I don't know if this book will ever leave the confines of my laptop computer, but if it does, and if by some miracle it should fall into the hands of any member of The Violent Femmes, I would just like to say, thanks guys, that was a blast.

At the end of the three weeks it is time to go back to California. Quickly. Braveheart, not fully grasping the size of the North American continent or perhaps just simply being a dick, booked a gig in Monterey one day after the last Violent Femmes date in Chicago. Even driving straight through the night it will be tough getting to the show on time.

To make matters worse, during our Great Lakes extravaganza the van has developed an indescribable funk. The smell subtly permeates the upholstery, the rubber floor mats and even the bare steel walls. It is an aromatic cocktail of fart, morning breath, arm pit, and week-old Egg McMuffin with just a hint of cheese-curd vomit. A discerning nose might also detect subtle overtones of ball sweat and bong water mopped up with a fungus-stained gym sock. We endure six relentless hours in the noxious atmosphere before unanimously concluding that we have time to stop at a car wash.

Somewhere in some town in the western third of the United States we find one of those coin operated affairs with manual scrub brushes. Everyone ponies-up their change and we diligently scrub until the paint is coming off, inside and out. We remove floor mats, trash, and ancient French fries from between the seat cushions. Laundry bags are stuffed into sealed suitcases. Any aroma-generating substance is either fully sanitized or thrown away. Finally, satisfied that The Funk has been fully banished, we pile in and hit the road.

All is well for the next 100 miles or so, driving through the night. Bruce is at the wheel with Bill riding shotgun. It's Bill's job to punch Bruce in the arm every 15 minutes to insure he doesn't fall asleep. Whenever the van jostles me awake, I kick the back of Bill's seat to make sure he's punching Bruce at the appropriate intervals.

Meanwhile, JT asks, "Are you awake Bruce?" every 10 minutes or so, effectively guaranteeing that we are all awake pretty much all the time.

The Funk returns at about 2:00 am. Despite our ingenious anti-nod-off system, we are all dozing at the time, even Bruce. He denies falling asleep at the wheel, but we are clearly on the shoulder within six inches of the guard rail when The Funk rouses us all like smelling salts.

"Good God," says JT as Bruce swerves from guard rail, "it smells like Bigfoot ate a plate of nachos, took a massive dump, then died. How can it be worse than it was before?"

We theorize on the source, its inhuman quality, and its potentially carcinogenic properties. But despite the olfactory discomfort and Bruce's protestations to the contrary, we soon all land on the same conclusion: The Funk saved our lives. A few more seconds and we would have smashed through that guard rail and flipped over the embankment 20 or 30 times, ending up like five eggs in a martini shaker. The Funk, it seems, is a benevolent force in our tiny universe. Though never fully able to embrace its presence wholeheartedly, the associations become nonetheless positive.

The Funk is the smell of home.

Twenty hours later we arrive at Doc's in Monterey, sleep deprived but alive. The club's full name is Doc Rickett's Lab, and like so many other venues of the time, it's downstairs in an unventilated basement. The peeling flat-black paint contributes to the hole-like quality of the place, but it's our hole, and we love it.

"Too High" is still number one at the local radio station and a line has formed around the block. I smile at the thought of our first show at Doc's a couple years earlier. Two waitresses and the bartender, Dino, were the only human beings in the place. After the show, which was really just a rehearsal due to the lack of an audience, Dino brought us round after round of Yeager shots, a mildly toxic liquid that tastes like cough syrup mixed with death.

A sign above the bar read, "Drinking triples until seeing double and acting single."

Dino, who also owned the bar, loved the band despite our lack of draw. He had us back every month since then until we built up the scene that currently stretched around the corner.

Mia and Eris drove down for the show together from San Francisco. Eris had befriended Mia long before I had acquired enough nads to bust a move. In fact, Eris did her best to help my cause early on, subtly laying the groundwork with subliminal suggestions like, "You should be fucking my brother."

As usual Eris stakes out her territory right up against the stage in front of JT's mic. Here she will gyrate seductively for her husband while flashing the occasional breast, a sight I try to avoid with my entire being. The phrase "sister-in-law" has the word "sister" built right in, so you catch my drift. The moment the music starts the capacity crowd rushes to the front, jostling and shoving for space. Eris, having dealt with this scenario since the Bogartz days, launches into The Elbow Dance, a routine she perfected over the years to ensure a modicum of real estate.

Deep into the set, during the bridge in "Bottle of Thunder," I notice that another girl upfront is obviously unimpressed with The Elbow Dance, most likely having been a recent recipient of its intended purpose. She is yelling and gesticulating but the words are no match for JT's Marshal nor Eris's complete indifference. I watch as the girl circles around, comes up behind Eris and shoves her with both hands into the stage.

Eris's face hits the base of JT's mic stand, sending the stand to the floor and bloodying Eris's nose. My brother, eyes wide with concern and fury, begins to remove his guitar in order to wade into the crowd for what will surely be a show-ending brawl, when Mia suddenly materializes, grabs the girl by the hair and drives a fist hard into the ol' breadbasket. Though at least 30 pounds heavier than Mia, the girl doubles over allowing Mia to clamp her neck in an unbreakable headlock. With her free hand Mia summons security, and two yellow jackets wade in for an old school heave-ho.

I am awestruck. My little Mia, peace loving yogini and friend of the homeless, shuts down a bar fight with a single upper cut to the diaphragm. Bill and Bruce are still holding down the rhythm while JT surveys the scene in complete disbelief.

I step up next to my brother and shout over the jackhammer rhythm, "By the way, I am marrying that girl!"

Mia lies on my shoulder beneath the boiled sheets of our darkened Super 8 motel room. My ears still ring while my mind plays reruns of the evening's highlights. I'm not sure if she's still awake, but my curiosity won't rest.

"I wonder if Paramahansa Yogananda would consider your actions tonight as less than yogic?"

She stirs and wraps her leg around mine. "Paramahansa wasn't Sicilian," she says.

"Maybe you invented a new pose? Doubled-Over Dog?"

"My father used to say, 'Niente è più importante della famiglia'—Nothing is more important than family."

"I can go with that, but let's face it, Eris kinda had it coming. She can be a bit of a bitch after a few Yeager shots. And besides, those elbows look sharp."

Mia sits up on her elbow, puts her hand on my cheek, and looks straight into my eyes. "Niente è più importante della famiglia."

Two weeks later we are back on the road, roaming the country with K's Choice, currently enjoying the success of "Not an Addict," when word comes down from the Glass Tower in New York: we have a release date for the album. I breath an inner sigh of relief, but the Record Company giveth, and the Record Company taketh away. The release date falls on the exact same date as Mia and my wedding, and promotional efforts will require a postponement.

I know Mia will face the news with a stoic half-smile and a downcast "that's ok," the thought of which I find utterly soul crushing. The good news, however, is that the textile industry offers a wide array of emergency engagement postponement support items. Mia recently fell in love with a knee length leather jacket, which ironically costs more than an entire live cow. I figured if I used the last of my credit card and did some serious busking on the Warf, I might be able to soften the blow with a little cow hide. ("Busking" is playing on the street for tips. On the scale of human destitution, it falls right between pan handling and dumpster diving).

During the set break in Austin, Texas I resolve to call Mia with the news. Having secured the essential gin 'n tonic and a pocket full of quarters, I make my way to the bar's pay phone and pick up the receiver, but a tap on my shoulder draws my attention away.

"Do chew g-g-guys know 'Free Bird?'" slurs a drunk patron.

"I don't," I answer, "but I think my brother does. He's right over there..."

Leaning in about three inches from my face he says, "Would you guys do a song I wrote?" The alcohol level of his breath is enough to completely sterilize my face. I could get a nose job right now without any surgical preparation.

Tilting my head back to the furthest extent of the phone cord I answer, "I'm sure my brother would be very interested. He's right over there..."

Oblivious to my response, he starts singing: "My love for you baby is like warm molasses/I wanna' wear you like a pair of sunglasses—"

"Uh-huh," I interrupt. "That's something my brother would really like. He's right over there..."

"Come on honey, don't make me beg/I love it when you take off your artificial leg..."

The last few verses fade into the background as I abandon the bar phone and head for the door. Passing the doorman, a meaty fist removes the G&T from my hand—love is sacrifice—and I head for the gas station across the street. A pay phone awaits among the diesel fumes.

Picking up the receiver, I pump my quarters into the slot and rapidly punch in the number. It takes unusually long to connect, but I finally hear a faint voice on the other end.

"Yah?"

"Hi Baby, it's me."

"Gjorde du verkligen bara Google denna mening?"

"What? Who is this?"

"Fyrkantiga hamburgare är djävulens patty..."

Just then a computerized voice breaks in, "Please deposit $50 for the next three minutes."

Oh my god, I miss-dialed and blew the bank roll on a call to Sweden. Good thing I have plastic. I hang up to try again when I notice my feet have become soaked. Looking up I see a woman at the pump madly battling a runaway hose while a 20-foot stream of gasoline coats a Lexus and a few customers heading into the mini-mart. Back in high school, my Health and Safety teacher would have described this as a "hazardous environment," so I hang up and head for the 7-Eleven next door.

Two pay phones stand by the entrance. I pick up the first one, but there's no dial tone. In fact, there's no cord between the receiver and the actual phone. I pick up the second one. Great! It works. I stab at the keypad but the first number sticks and the button won't spring back. Bits of old chocolate and what appears to be hardened vanilla ice cream cake the phone. In my mind's eye I see a man yelling into the receiver until—in a final act of frustration—he crams a perfectly good Dove Bar into the keypad. I would get one myself—if I had any quarters left.

Fine. I survey the area and notice a phone booth on the corner at the end of the block. Five minutes left in the break. I dash down the sidewalk, step up to the booth, and push on the door. It won't open. I pull on the door. It won't open. I rattle it. Nothing. I kick it. Nope.

I pound it with my fist when unexpectedly it folds open in that weird way that phone booths open and I fall into that V-shaped crevice which causes the two sides to squish together with my face between them, so I jerk back and get my sleeve caught on the handle which causes the doors to really slam shut and jam twice as hard as before. I go completely ballistic on the phone both. I kick it, swear at it, pound it, shoulder slam it... Everything but *open* it.

Defeated and out of time I sulk back to the club.

If Mia was upset, she gave no sign. She loved the leather consolation prize, but I could tell it wasn't necessary. We simply put an "X" on the next page of the calendar and continued to plan the wedding. The second postponement, due to yet another shift in the release date, was met with an accepting "shit happens" smile. The third postponement was as easy as the previous two, but when the forth postponement hit, I saw something in Mia's expression that caused a physical tear in my soul: doubt.

"You know," she said with the sweetest pragmatism, "maybe we shouldn't worry about getting married right now. We can plan it for another time, maybe when things settle down."

She was giving me a way out, an escape hatch. How could she believe that this was something I wanted?

No. We set a date and that date was final. I made some calls. I dug in. I put the word out that *this* wedding date was an immobile pillar of concrete sunk into the core of the Earth. There would be no fifth postponement.

Except there was.

A record's release date at a major label is a mysterious amalgamation of departments, tour schedules, personalities and Ouija Board guesswork. Our record would drop on a Tuesday with about 10 other releases. Most records get four to six weeks of promotion effort to see which one gains traction. The most promising of those releases gets the full might of the machine behind them, while the rest are quietly loaded into the dumpsters out back.

Not a lot of intuition was necessary to foresee a future in which both my relationship and my album would wind up in a landfill but taking a stand against the record company at this point would be catastrophic for everyone involved. The band, their families, and all our support folks were all standing at the edge of this cliff with Mia and I. One wrong move and we all go over the edge.

A couple of sleepless nights later I go for the Hail Mary.

"Would you be heartbroken," I say to Mia, "if we were to forget the big wedding and just fly to Maui and get the job done?"

A month later, surrounded by our closest friends and family on Ulua Beach in Maui, I steal the most precious jewel ever held in The Vault of Impossibility.

Mia is mine.

And God Said: Nothing Special

"Start with the basics
Just be nice
And see if that makes things alright"
- What God Said, The Uninvited

"'What God Said' is going to be the biggest single of 1998..."

"Our whole third quarter is riding on The Uninvited..."

"I hope you guys are ready for the big time..."

The hype coming from all directions knocked us off our feet like a bullshit riot hose. Though jaded enough to know better, distracting flecks of gold in the verbal detritus focused our attention. Influential stations in Las Vegas, Dallas, Austin, and New York added the first single, "What God Said," and audiences were responding.

But the biggest prize was feedback from KROQ in Los Angeles, the station that defined alternative rock for the rest of the nation. A blessing from KROQ would swing wide the gates to Rock Heaven. The Program Director was confident the song was a hit, scheduling it to be added in the next week.

In support of the radio play, we pile in the van and head for the vast desert expanses of the Southwest. Our first show of the tour is at Trees in Dallas, Texas, opening for Fuel, currently killing it with their first major label single, "Shimmer."

The venue is oversold, and the promoter asks if we would be willing to do two shows that night.

"Does that mean we get twice the money?" we ask.

A long, rambling response weaves and spins around the ticket office filled with hundreds more syllables than one might expect for a simple "no," but somewhere in the commentary the words "free drinks" stand out, so we accept.

We take the stage for our first set, but I forgot my hat. I come to the realization about three songs in when a stray hair begins to tickle my lower lip. I'm screwed. Can't move it, can't scratch it, can't do anything but try to blow it out of the way while my hands work the guitar. It won't move. Somehow, the hair is solidly suspended above my lip and I can't stop thinking about it. The tickle turns to annoyance, then aggravation, then pure torment, and I begin to consider a full face-plant into the carpeting on the floor of the stage.

That's it, I can't take it. I steel my nerves to wipe my face on Bill's grotesquely sweaty back when an acidic bolt of white-hot pain burns into my left eye as the first bead of sweat rolls down and penetrates the thin defense of my eyelash. It's that cheap Motel 6 conditioner.

The active ingredient must be hydrochloric acid because I can literally feel my eye fizzing away like an Alka-Seltzer dropped in water. Now the sweat hits my right eye and I'm totally blind. My eyes are melting in their sockets and the residue is running down my cheekbones as if I were in some grade B horror movie. I can't see anyone or anything. Oh God, the chorus is coming up ... Where's the mic? I can't see the mic ... The guys are going to be pissed that I missed my part ... Where's my fucking hat?

The chorus comes and goes without my backing vocal. I'm supposed to be singing "All my young and beautiful friends," an ironic line in context of the song made doubly incongruous by my own lack of beauty. I must look pretty cool stumbling around the stage with my eyes running down my face. Now I feel my hair falling forward, completely enshrouding my entire head. I picture how the crowd sees me: is that guy wearing a bell over his head?

I really miss my hat.

I'm perched on the edge of a complete break down when by shear chance I accidentally bump into the microphone. The mic! I'm saved! And just in time for the next chorus. I take a deep breath in preparation to belt out the first line, and suck about a foot of hair right down my throat. The acidic hairball clogs my larynx, and the first line of the chorus comes out as "Ugahchkchch..."

Suddenly, I'm thankful for my blindness: I can't see the glaring faces of my bandmates, who will later have me as the guest of honor at an ass kicking party after the show.

The thought of my eminent beating, however, is quickly drowned out by a growing need for oxygen. The hairball has completely blocked my windpipe and all attempts to cough it up in a cat-like fashion prove fruitless. I'm looking forward to passing out. Bring on the blackness, baby, anything to end the torment. I realize now that when they send me to hell, they won't let me pack my hat.

I need an old school MTV Hair Moment. I'll just lean way, way forward, then throw my head back. My mass of hair will yank out of my throat and swing backwards in a cool arc just like a bitchin rock star with sweat flying in the multi-colored lights. I go for it. I fling my head back with incredible force and...

Yes, it works! I can breathe!

Greedily I suck in a big gulp of air, but something is amiss. I can't move my head. In fact, my body is still bent backwards, and I can't stand up straight. Out of the corner of my eye the situation becomes clear: all my hair is now tangled in the headstock of JT's guitar – not the bitchin rock star moment I was hoping for.

JT and I attempt to untangle the mess as the song rages on, but we only manage to put his guitar drastically out of tune. As my hair winds around his tuning pegs, part of my mind begins to compose the ad I'll soon be placing in the local music papers back home: "Guitarist, recently booted for inability to control his hair, seeks new project..."

Finally, the song mercifully peters out to a sloppy, discordant end. Scattered golfers' applause trickles through the thoroughly unimpressed crowd as Our Man Tony guides me off with JT's guitar hanging from my head.

"Oh man," says Tony as he tries to unravel the mess backstage, "Is there a 911 for hairstylists?"

Blinded, all I can say is, "Have you seen my hat?"

Tony procures a baseball cap from Fuel's merch booth. Our Marketing Department has yet to materialize, so all we sell are t-shirts and CDs.

"Here ya go, that's your dinner budget for tomorrow," says Tony.

I set the cap on backwards, hoping I don't look too much like a jerkoff frat boy, and settle in to watch Fuel's set.

They spit. A lot.

Their sound is much more punk than their single would suggest, which would account for the spitting. Singer Brett Scallions hawks one into the air and deftly catches it back in his mouth. He repeats the maneuver several times, eliciting a ripple of approval from the crowd. I marvel at the thought that I work in a field where launching and catching a wad of phlegm is a serviceable job skill. Should I be working on this? Do I need to add Mucus Juggling to my skill set?

The next discharge goes astray. It's understandable, a lot of moving parts comprise a rock show and the introduction of airborne saliva is going to further complicate matters. The wayward loogie arches unexpectedly to the right. Initially I judge its descent will put it harmlessly on the floor, but the bass player, unaware of the in-flight bile, repositions himself to exactly the wrong spot presenting his left cheek as the only possible landing site.

The impact takes him unawares. Allowing the root note to sustain, he wipes his cheek and inspects the offending material in his palm. A look of disgust ripples over his face. His eyes flash up to the singer with pure hatred. I suspect this is not a first-time occurrence. The defiled bass player makes a show of wiping his palm on his pants, never removing his gaze from the singer. Though no further altercation ensues, I suspect their van ride back to the hotel tonight will be a little awkward.

Our second set goes much smoother than the first. I look like I'm on my way to a kegger with the bros, but at least my hair is contained. We work hard to win over the crowd as the show progresses, pulling liberally from our bag of tricks accumulated over the last eight years. Gradually, cautiously they give up the love. I want the relationship to go faster, but understand that this is, after all, our first date.

Finally, we come to the last song of the set. In the time-honored tradition of every rock concert since 1955 we saved the radio hit for last. JT fires up the distorted intro to "What God Said," but we are unprepared for what happens next: Silence. Every conversation in the club stops in mid-sentence. The only sound I hear is JT's guitar.

In eerie unison every face in the room turns toward the band. But when Bill and Bruce deliver the gut punch, the joint explodes. People rush the stage from the back of the room, banging heads and pumping fists.

They know this song.

They love this song.

They came here and paid money for this moment.

So this is the power of radio, I think to myself. Radio makes the introductions, greases the tracks, lays all the groundwork long before you come to town. Radio infuses your song into the everyday lives of people until your voice is familiar and comforting like shooting the breeze with an old friend.

Radio is everything.

Over the course of the next week we work our way back to California, pulling all-nighters in front of sparse crowds in tiny bars located in towns whose names are printed so small on our map they are indecipherable to the naked eye. In most of these places we were complete unknowns, providing background music for lonely divorcées and middle-aged men who didn't want to go home. Often times we were just competition for the television over the bar. On one particular night we were so incapable of turning attention away from the TV we finally gave up, sat down on the edge of the stage, and checked out the season finale of *X-Files* with everyone else. The manager didn't even notice, paying us our $500 at the end of the night without question.

One illegible dot on our *Thomas Brothers Map* connects to the next until we finally roll into Northern California, eager to join with Chris Isaak for a series of gigs along the West Coast. The first few shows take place at a venue called The Mountain Winery in Saratoga. It's a stunning outdoor amphitheater with panoramic views of the surrounding wine country, tucked in a picturesque grove of redwood trees. The crisp air smells of oak, pine and gentrification.

I have never felt our band name was more appropriate than the moment we started loading in backstage. This would be our first exposure to the wine and cheese crowd, and it made me a little nervous. Chris Isaak was an amazing crooner whose velvet falsetto is the perfect complement to a full-bodied cabernet sauvignon. The Uninvited pair nicely with Pabst Blue Ribbon and a DUI.

On the first night we decide to play it safe, breaking out acoustic guitars and presenting our whitest, most brie-like material. The ending of each song is met with a ripple of hesitant applause, as everyone had to set down their stemware every three-and-a-half minutes to politely pat their palms.

This state of affairs would not do.

The second night we roll out the Marshalls and Mesa Boogie amps, plug in and unleash a full-frontal set. The crowd looks a little wind-blown after the first song, but three or four numbers into it the little cheese plates have fallen to the floor and audience is on their feet.

We plow through 45 minutes of melodic distortion and end the set to calls for an encore, but it's not to be. No sooner does the last chord fade than Chris' road manager storms the stage visibly pissed. He starts chucking cables off into the wings and rolls out amps with an indignant shove.

Our drummer attempts to calm the situation with a little Bruce-style diplomacy, "Dude, don't be such a dick," which only serves to increase the magnitude of dickishness.

Conversely, when we stroll into the backstage area, Chris himself is all smiles.

"Hey fellas, that was really a great set," he says shaking our hands. He is handsome to an unsettling extent, blessed with genetics that give him a Darwinian advantage in this particular ecosystem. Moreover, he has enough money to surround himself with a shield of assholes, so he doesn't have to be one himself. In a profession where knives protrude from countless backs, Chris can afford to be a nice guy.

We thank him profusely for his kind words regarding our set while eyeing a deli tray with markedly superior cheese selections.

More pleasantries are exchanged when he asks an unexpected question: "Let's say someone came to you with a song that was a guaranteed hit. A song so good that you knew in your heart it would go to number one, but it's from an outside writer. Would you do the song?"

"Probably not," says JT. "We're really into doing our own stuff."

"Yeah," I agree. "I just can't see an outside writer being able to connect with our sound."

"You guys should think about that," says Chris with a smile. "One song, just one big hit song, is all you need to make a living making music for the rest of your life."

"Hopefully we have that song," says JT.

"Hopefully," repeats Chris as he strolls out to prepare for his set.

Just as Chris leaves the room, Eris, Mia, and Mia's friend, Julie, walk in with All Access laminates accessorizing tiny cocktail dresses and spikey heels. The venue is only a two-hour drive from the East Bay and the girls are eager to see us in such genteel surroundings. JT and Eris envelope one another before discreetly evaporating. I make a mental note that the bathroom will be unavailable for the next 10 minutes or so.

As Mia swoops in for a longer than usual kiss I regret that JT and Eris got to the bathroom first. I contemplate the easy accessibility of Mia's tiny dress when we hear Chris' band fire up, so we head out to watch.

He's killing it. The band is tight, and one hit follows the next. Not only does Chris carry himself like a star, he literally sparkles like a star. The entire surface area of his suit is covered in tiny glass mirrors, like a human disco ball, which reflect a thousand beams of light into the crowd.

Around mid-set, while introducing the band members, a loud crash booms backstage. The noise is so jarring everyone in Chris' band turns their head toward the black curtain separating the stage from backstage. I pass a worried glance to Mia and jog up the loading dock stairs.

Backstage I find Eris and Julie heaped on the floor, incapacitated in drunken laughter and surrounded by broken wine glasses.

"Are you guys okay?" I ask, wading through the glass minefield.

They manage to nod in the affirmative though still unable to speak through the laughter. Certain that we have incurred the wrath of Chris' handlers, I help them both up while mapping out the quickest retreat through the glass.

"Okay ladies, we're going to need to get the hell out of here before the Stage Manager shows up. Trust me, he's not a fun guy."

We step lively from the scene until I find Tony and relinquish the girls to his care.

The next day we get a call from our agent, Kevin. I have the misfortune of picking up the mobile.

"What the fuck?" says Kevin.

Clever and quick witted I have the perfect retort:

"Uh..."

"Not only did you break five cases of wine glasses you interrupted their performance. Who does that? Who could be that incredibly stupid?"

"Um..." I say, once again wielding the razor-sharp edge of my intellect.

"Whatever. The end result is they dropped you from the tour. You guys are out. I'm sorry."

"Damn Kevin, I'm sorry too. I don't know what to say. There was an issue backstage, but I suspect we may have been a little much for the soccer-mom-and-chardonnay crowd anyway."

"Yeah, it's cool," he says simmering down. "You're right, it wasn't a great fit. Don't worry, I'll come up with something."

That night, when I break the news to JT over a couple of gin 'n tonics, he looks more contemplative than upset.

"Remember what Chris told us about outside songwriters?" he says. "What if Chris had a particular song he wanted us to do? What if *he* wrote a song that would fit with us? What if it was the perfect song that would propel us to the top? What if he had the next 'Free Bird' or 'Stairway to Heaven'...?"

"I guess we'll never know," I say.

"Nope," says JT with a carefree smile, clinking his glass against mine. "No use crying over spilled opportunity."

"That's for sure. We'd be swimming in it by now."

With the newly created gap in our schedule, Atlantic summons us to their pristine, hallowed offices in Los Angeles for "Press Day," where we will be interviewed by pubescent journalism interns working for B-list "Zines." (In the 1990's, Zines were the analog version of what would eventually become Blogs).

Frank Zappa once said, "Most rock journalism is people who can't write, interviewing people who can't talk, for people who can't read."

After the first five or six interviews it becomes clear that only two questions enflame the curiosity of contemporary rock journalists: "How did you get your name?" and "What are your musical influences?"

I will give you the answer to the first one just in case you missed that copy of *Suburban Death March* at your local news stand.

In the early days of the band we had a list. Entry to the apartment required a band name be added to that list regardless of whether you lived there or not. Quality was not a consideration, nor originality. We just wanted the first words that popped into your mind. Every phone call, every conversation, every interaction with a human being required a name be added to the list.

The final choosing of the name was postponed for months until our first gig required we be called something. An in-depth analysis of our options revealed that we had collected 10 pages of shit. No one could agree on a single name. Of all the names on the list, however, one stood out as the worst. Since the only consensus we could summon was that all of us did *not* like the name "The Uninvited," we decided that should be our name. Second runner up was "Dead Cats on a Fence," but Bill thought it was kinda cool, so it got tossed.

Not only did all the young Jann Wenners come equipped with the same questions, they all had a similar look behind their eyes that I couldn't quite figure out at first. After two or three interviews it became clear that the look was really a question, something that they burned to ask but couldn't find a way to frame: *Should I be impressed?*

Everyone wants to be in the presence of celebrity, but this pre-celebrity stage was confusing, a potential that could go either way. We were being assessed for cool by teenage gatekeepers, desperate to figure out if their own peers would love them for loving us.

After a punishing morning of drool-inducing repetitive interviews, the receptionist walked in clutching a pizza. Hallelujah, lunch time.

"Here you go!" she said with an oversized smile. Is there anything else I can do for you boys?" She bent over to show us the pizza giving full effect to her low-cut blouse.

I couldn't be totally sure but judging by the look on her face many-a-musician had all kinds of needs fulfilled on this very conference table.

"Sure," I replied leaning back from the potentially tainted surface, "could we get a massive prophylactic to cover this table before you put that pizza down?"

"I have one that will fit rolled up in the back of the van," said JT. "I have to have them custom made."

"Um," mumbled the receptionist with the confused look of someone contemplating where they might find a giant table condom.

"It's cool," I said. "We're all good."

That evening our Product Manager, David, takes the band and our managers out to dinner at a restaurant on Sunset Blvd. It has a six-month waiting list for everyone except David. I never get a coherent read on what exactly David's job is, but it appears that he fluffs life's pillows for the label's artists, like a kinder, gentler A&R guy.

When the waiter comes by, we don't get menus. David places an order for the table off the top of his head to spare us the agony of having to make a decision. A few cocktails later, gigantic plates containing tiny clusters of edible art land in front of us. It's something French and tastes the way an impressionist masterpiece looks.

After dinner, out in the parking lot, Arthur Spivak pulls us aside. "I have bad news," he says. "We are not going to get the add at KROQ."

"Well, they wanted Tori to play at the KROQ festival. She wanted to be paid for her performance even though traditionally big stations don't pay artists to play at their events. KROQ said no pay, so she refused the gig. The station got mad, dropped her from the playlist and is refusing to play anyone associated with her, including you guys. I am so sorry, but she won't budge on the issue. She believes it is a matter of principle, and I stand with her."

"Shit," says Bill. "It's great that Tori wants to take a stand and everything but for us it's a steaming hot bowl of Cream of Fucked soup."

I put a hand on Bill's shoulder. "It's okay," I say as an idea takes form. All we need to do is get face to face with Tori for a few minutes, have Bruce do some professional listening to her side of the story, then send in JT to close the deal with some of that enchanting hocus-pocus. We can turn this shit wagon around in the course of 30 minutes.

"Arthur," I say, "can you arrange a meeting with Tori and us?"

"No."

"Really? I think we could help all of us here with just a few minutes..."

"No."

"But if she fully understood..."

"I'm sorry but I can't. Tori is an extremely private person and does not want any pressure from outside sources."

Arthur has the dismissive look of someone who has left the subject, and we retreat to our own thoughts. My first inclination is to find her, but resources to that effect are limited. These are the days before the Internet would divulge the ovulation frequency of your favorite pop star, or anything else you wanted to know. The band had an AOL account, but that was only good for email and chatrooms where fart obsessed 10-year-olds were practicing to become the full-fledge trolls of today. Tori is out of reach, and our chances of creating a hit are slipping away.

"Don't worry guys," Arthur says with a tone of reassurance. "The song is doing well at several prominent stations. It's number 3 in Tulsa, Oklahoma, and you guys are playing a big festival there next week. If we push it to number one, we'll definitely have Atlantic's attention. We can save this thing."

Two short days after dropping me off at home, the van pulls up again with its familiar horn and sliding door. I kiss Mia goodbye and grab my duffle bag. "Have fun in Chicago," I say over my shoulder.

Mia took a job with Land Rover as a Product Specialist. Now she flies all over the country to attend car shows, handing out brochures while explaining to suburban moms why they need an SUV built for the African Savana to drive kids to the mall.

When she first got the job, I asked her, "Do you do this in a bathing suit holding a lion's leash next to the car on a rotating stage? Because that would be pretty hot." She gave me The Eyebrow.

"No," she said. "I am supposed to wear kakis and a pith helmet, but I got them to ditch the hat."

"Good," I said. "Nothing hot about The Jungle Cruise look, unless the hat is the only thing you're wearing ... but in that case you should ask for more money."

"The job title is 'Product Specialist' not 'Stripper'—no lion, no rotating stage, no nudity, no pole, just brochures and information."

"Hmm. Won't get many tips."

"Don't need 'em. My husband's a rock star."

A sweet sentiment but I wasn't exactly bringing home the bacon. My contribution was more like bacon bits. All other food, smoked meats and otherwise, was provided through the considerable efforts of my wife. Mia kept the lights on while I swung for the homerun.

I did a great job of envisioning myself as the mighty hunter, spear in hand, trudging across the frozen tundra in search of the Wooly Mammoth. You bring one of those massive bastards back to the cave and it's a full year of mammoth steaks and furry slippers for everyone. But meanwhile, Mia is keeping the home fires burning and providing real, tangible food. Not potential food.

Those considerable efforts, and my appreciation for them, weigh on my mind as I walk out to the van.

"Hey, Goatee Man, take me with you."

I glance up to see my neighbor's ceramic garden gnome permanently reclining on a tiny park bench overlooking their lawn. A mammoth plastic dragonfly is attached to the bench above his head. Though I am sure the desired effect is pastoral tranquility, the dragon fly gives the scene a disquieting primordial feel.

"Jesus Christ this bug is boring the shit out me. If I gotta spend one more day with its goddamn wing in my face I'm gonna blow my brains out." The Gnome paused. *"Oh wait, that's right, I can't, because my fucking arms don't move. Dude. Help a brother out. Take me with you."*

I smile but dismiss the thought as I climb into the van. *"Wait!"* calls The Gnome. *"I'll be your good luck charm! You've heard about leprechauns and pots of gold and shit, right? Dude, you need me!"*

"Wait a minute Tony," I say. I dash back into the house, scribble down a quick note, and kiss Mia on my way out. I do a quick survey of the 'hood—no one around—sprint across the street, grab the statue, drop the note in his place and dart back into the van.

"What's this?" asks Tony.

"It's a garden gnome," I say placing his permanently reclining body on the dashboard. "He's going to bring us good luck."

The first show of the tour is in Las Vegas, another city where the song is doing well. This is our first all-ages show since we signed to Atlantic, and a New Orleans band called Cowboy Mouth is the opener. Though we have never seen the band before our agent raves about them. He says Fred LeBlanc, the band's lead singer and drummer, is one of the greatest showmen in the business.

We meet the guys backstage where the promoter's staff is serving lunch.

I reach out to shake Fred's hand. "How's it going, I'm Steve..."

Fred takes my hand, pulls me in close, and helps himself to an enormous bite of a sandwich I'm holding in my other hand. "I'm Fred," he says spitting crumbs all over both our shirts.

As JT steps up, Fred turns, reaches down, and grabs himself a generous handful of my brother's ass. "Wow!" he says, "You're a big fella!" JT is about one full guitar length taller than Fred.

"That's right!" says JT. "You could blow me without even getting on your knees."

Uh oh.

The room goes quiet. Not a promising start to the tour.

But it turns out, as usual, JT knew what he was doing—Fred bursts into laughter. "Oh my god, I LOVE this guy!" he says, giving JT's ass an extra squeeze.

The tension snaps and we all settle into chatting, drinking, and swapping war stories. We find out their lead guitarist, Griff, was a founding member of the Red Rockers back in the 80's, sending Bill into a fanboy crush:

"Holy shit you're John Thomas Griffith! I grew up on you man! I mean, not actually on you, but, you know, like, well, shit, you're John Thomas Griffith!"

The party goes on until show time when Fred and company

stroll out on to the stage.

Our agent was right. Fred rocks the house like a wrecking ball. They set up his drum kit front-of-stage, and he pulls out every stick twirling trick in the book. Short and stocky, he's a Cajun rhythm pile-driver delivering a creole-seasoned beating to everyone in the room. At one point Fred calls over his drum tech, Eddie, and working one stick at a time, hands over the kit mid-song without missing a beat.

Fred is not happy about people in their seats. He grabs the wireless mic out of the stand and wades into the crowd grabbing arms of the wallflowers, pulling the shy or disengaged up onto the dance floor. "Come on people! Are you WITH ME?"

One kid, however, is not with him. He stays affixed to his seat, bored and indifferent, despite all of Fred's cajoling.

"Break it down," Fred says to the band. The beat drops to a single kick drum hitting quarter notes while the volume takes a precipitous dive.

"Hey buddy," Fred announces on the mic to the kid, "I really need you get UP!"

The entire audience is watching the scene now, but the kid just looks away.

"Dude, I'm going to have to do my special microphone dance if you don't get out of that chair."

The kid slouches further into his seat.

"Are you sure you wanna do this?" asks Fred.

Sublime indifference from the kid.

"Ok, here goes!"

He shimmies up onto the teenager's seat until he's straddling the disinterested adolescent with a foot on each arm rest. Holding the mic between his legs he thrusts with his hips tapping the mic head against the kid's forehead in time to the kick drum. I'm expecting the teen to start swinging but he just closes his eyes and turns his head while the mic pounds the rhythm to "Jenny Says" against his cheek.

Watching side-stage JT comments, "That's a good two or three grand in future therapy sessions right there."

Cowboy Mouth gets two encores before finally wrapping up, leaving the audience spent. I can't remember the last time an opener ate our lunch, but we are truly upstaged. We will be with our Louisiana friends for the next few nights, and we will be watching. Great artists steal only from the best, and I make a mental note to study every move Fred makes over the next few shows.

Though we have to work for it we manage to make an impression on the exhausted crowd. As usual the radio hit does the heavy lifting for us, and I'm grateful for the slight advantage. After the show we gather at the merch booth to sign CDs, t-shirts, or whatever.

I lean against the table, shaking hands and feeling somewhat awkward. After all these years I still don't know how to respond to compliments and admiration that far surpass my own self-assessment. I once read that in the back of every tour bus is a fraud terrified of being exposed.

A girl approaches me with the band's t-shirt and a sharpie pen. She's somewhere between 16 and 26-years-old, I can never tell, especially when they dress like *that*.

"Will you sign this for me?" she says with an excited smile.

"Sure," I say, taking the shirt and looking for some place flat. She turns around and offers her back. I lay the t-shirt on her shoulders, and she bends over slightly, tucking her butt into my crotch and nuzzling it up firmly.

I draw a quick "Steve" and back away, handing her the shirt at arm's length.

"So, what are you doing after this?" she asks.

"Oh, I'm just gonna go back to the hotel, by myself, and be ... you know ... married."

"Would you like some company?" she asks, either missing or dismissing the point.

"Excuse me," I say, leaving the merch table to retreat out the back door. I walk out to the van and escape into the safety of the passenger seat, having experienced enough human interaction for one night.

"*What the hell was that?*" asks The Gnome. I look out window as the last of the concert goers trickle out of the theater. "*Joe Perry would bitch slap you and take away your guitar picks.*"

I'm overcome with the urge to take my sharpie and drive it through his eye, but I restrain myself.

I summon the Inner Buddha.

He settles into the driver seat, rolls of flesh spilling over the edges of the chair. He takes a long, deep pull from a Bob Marley-sized joint and passes it to The Gnome. The Gnome takes a hit and passes it back to the Buddha, who then holds it out to me. I reach for the splif but the Buddha jams the cherry into the back of my hand singeing the flesh between my thumb and forefinger.

"You know what Gnome?" I say shaking my hand, "Fuck you. Yeah, I could have that girl, but what's the point? The whole time I would be imagining the girl I would rather be with. And when it's over, I would lose what I really wanted in the first place."

"*No you wouldn't,*" says The Gnome, "*It's not like you have to set up a billboard, 'Hey I fucked a groupie in Vegas!' No one has to know...*"

"Yeah, no one but *me*. Fuck off."

After a week of battling for Stage Supremacy with Cowboy Mouth it is time to part ways with our new friends from New Orleans. We gather at a Denny's for one last breakfast to say goodbye. Over bowls of over-cooked oatmeal and under-cooked Grand Slams, Fred tells us about a game a fellow New Orleans band used to play called, "Fuck the Pig."

Though he liberally sprinkles the tale with vivid biological details, rendering our eggs inedible, the basic concept is that the band has to buy breakfast for the member who brings the ugliest girl to breakfast. The game's ethical shortcomings are debated for a while, but it is generally agreed that "Fuck the Pig" won't make the list of pastimes for either band.

After breakfast we shake hands in the parking lot and pile into our respective vehicles. Our Man Tony tells me to make a left out of the lot, and finally we are on our way to the biggest, most important show of the tour, the K-ROCK Festival in Tulsa, Oklahoma. But two hours later, excitement turns into incredulity and eventually panic-stricken horror as Tony comes to the realization that we have driven 150 miles in the opposite direction of the gig.

A 90-mile-per-hour excursion through all seven levels of Dante's Inferno ensues, ending in the fairgrounds one hour past our set time with both our trailer tire and our career engulfed in flames.

Ducking out the side door of the van, Bruce pours two bottles of what looks suspiciously like urine on the flaming tire, extinguishing the smoldering rubber in a cloud of noxious steam. The sigh of the dying fire is timed perfectly with the sigh escaping my own lips.

"You are too late," says Mustache Guy, "You'll need to change that tire and get this thing out of the loading area immediately." He turns and walks away before I can even begin any kind of groveling.

"*And that's when the band broke up and Steve became a feral homeless man with bubble gum dreadlocks and a trash bag loin cloth,*" mumbles The Gnome.

JT scrambles right over my lap and bursts through driver-side door. "Excuse me!" he calls after the Figure of Authority. The man does not slow his pace at all, but JT is on him in five long strides.

I watch as my brother matches his pace without impeding him, smiling all the while and speaking in what appears to be an amicable tone. Relaxed gestures are exchanged, slight nods, and finally a handshake.

Jogging back to the van JT calls out, "We're on next! Load that shit out!"

"Let me guess," I say grabbing a road case, "you validated his authority, verbally soothed his darkest insecurities, and allowed him to reaffirm his humanity by performing a small favor for us..."

"I threatened to drag him behind the van for the remainder of the tour if he didn't let us play," JT says grabbing the other side of the case. "Or maybe that was plan B? Whatever. We're on in 10 minutes."

The festival has two main stages. One band plays on one stage while the next band sets up on the other, thus keeping the show going at all times. In the history of The Uninvited there has never been a more focused, diligent, and efficient load in. Having performed this ritual almost every night for years we could set up our gear in a hurricane with bags over our heads. Amps land in place, plugs find sockets, jacks find inputs, guitars find stands and we are ready.

On the second stage Harvey Danger is careening through the last distorted chorus of their encore, "Flagpole Sitta." Our Man Tony picks up my guitar and holds the strap out ready to drape over my shoulder, an offering of penitence for past sins. I meet his eyes as he wraps me in the instrument.

"All good m' brother, we made it," I assure him.

He smiles back, but it is obvious it will be a while until he lets himself off the hook.

The comforting heft of my Gibson Les Paul grounds me physically and emotionally. Made from a solid block of 3-inch thick mahogany the Les Paul has landed many a guitarist on the chiropractic table, but I find the weight reassuring. These guitars are known for their sustain, the ability to hold a note out unimaginable lengths of time. Deep in the grain of this guitar a note from 1979 still resonates.

I discovered this particular instrument in a pawn shop in Austin, Texas. Old and worn, it carried a hundred scars and a thousand stories tellable only in the language of music. A single strum and the genie was out. At first, I was hesitant to buy it, not because it would require three month's rent money, but because I felt like I was taking someone else's lover. Vintage guitars don't end up in pawn shops because everything is going swell. On the other hand, every lover we take is someone else's broken heart. That's the cycle of love, and so this Gibson and I began our affair.

While T-Money plugs in my guitar cable Clipboard Guy endeavors to make himself noticed side-stage, arms spread wide in the universal "What the fuck?" stance. Harvey Danger had just wrapped up, and it's go time.

JT spins around to face the band screaming, "ONE TWO THREE FOUR!"

By virtue of the psychic connection that can only form through eight years of zero personal space, we all manage to hit the downbeat of "Mega Multi-Media Hero" despite the fact that we have no set list nor did we at any time discuss what we would play. JT's timing, the expression on his face, the position of his hand on his guitar—it was all we needed.

The audio punch created by one million watts of festival sound gear resets 20 thousand heartbeats like a massive sonic defibrillator. Within the first five seconds of the first song the sea of swaying bodies stretched out before us are all operating on the same wavelength.

The crowd is so deep and massive I can't see the back rows through the Oklahoma dust, but I know the blast of my A-chord is making conversation impossible for at least a two-mile radius. Up front the crowd pushes forward against the security barricades while Tulsa bouncers in yellow windbreakers toss would-be stage divers back in the crowd like feather pillows. As the audience pushes forward, we subconsciously step up to greet the throng until all our toes are hanging-ten off the front of the stage.

Looking to my left I see the bring-it-on expressions of Bill and JT, challenging the mob to close the gap.

All anyone ever really wants in life is to be loved. Money, success, power—they are all just perceived pathways to the root of our true desires: love and acceptance. What is the use of a bitchin Mercedes Benz if no one ever sees you in it? We all want to be revered members of the Tribe.

Think back to high school lunch-period, wandering around the cafeteria navigating the tables of jocks, cool kids, geeks, etc. until hopefully finding a seat where you would be welcome or at least tolerated. Now imagine that you stepped foot in that dank cafeteria and every kid in the place stood up on their seat screaming and pleading for you to come sit by them. The Prom Queen, the Quarterback, the President of the Chess Club, all of them begging to be next to you, to be seen with you, to love you.

That is what it feels like to connect with an audience.

On that summer evening standing on that Tulsa stage we are feeling the love, and it reflects off us right back on them in a continuous orgasmic feedback loop. One song rolls right into the next as we let go of the fear and frustration of our deathly trip to Fuckedville. We hammer out the material in cathartic precision with the confidence of eight years and six independent albums under our belts. But just when we really have them in a froth, Clipboard Guy gives the throat-slash hand signal signifying a blunt and brutal end to the set.

As the last chord rings out JT turns to the microphone: "Thank you, Tulsa, you guys are AWESOME! Have a great night!"

The audience responds, but the applause feels restrained, almost disappointed. I lifted the guitar from my shoulder and unconsciously tug at the cable, perplexed at the lack of enthusiasm. Tony steps up, always ready for the handoff, but his face is a new mask of agony.

"Oh Christ, what now?"

"The single man, you forgot the freakin single..."

The single. The hit. "What God Said," the whole reason we were invited to play this gig in the first place.

Have you ever been to a concert where the band didn't play that one song you paid the exorbitant ticket price to hear? The song you wait for, the song that makes you scream at the first note?

We didn't play it. The asshole population of Tulsa had just grown by four.

No one utters a word as we load the gear back into the trailer. I roll open the side door of the van to retrieve the tire jack when The Gnome breaks the silence.

"Whoa, nice job. How many times do you get the chance to disappoint 20,000 people all at the same time! That's like letting down all of your friends only multiplied by, in your case, 20,000."

"We were rushed ... flustered. We had no set list..." I say to the band or The Gnome, I'm not sure which.

Tony gets busy on the trailer tire while the rest of us sulk down to the Meet 'n Greet tent where the performers sign autographs.

Kids step through the line with t-shirts, CDs, packs of smokes, or beer cups to sign, all with the same question, "Why didn't you play 'What God Said'?"

The apologies pile up until we're drowning in penitence, gasping for the cool air outside the tent.

We bail.

On the way to the motel we push back on the dark mood, telling each other shit happens and laughing over the new burn marks on the right side of the trailer.

The next morning, we get word that the radio station dropped the single. An hour later Atlantic pulls the plug on "What God Said."

It's All Good

"Hey here comes Father Time
He's holding up a cardboard sign
Says any day might be the end now"
Is That Me – The Uninvited

After the last show of the tour, outside a tired Motel 6, Bill takes my arm before heading into the room: "Hey man, I gotta talk to you."

Motel 6 had a slogan: *"We'll leave the light on for you."* Tonight, that light is a harsh blue bug zapper exposing every dark circle and stress line on Bill's face.

"What's up?" I reply, surveying the deep trench running between his eyebrows.

"I just spoke with Kelly," he says.

Kelly is Bill's wife. I performed their marriage ceremony myself two years earlier. Having clipped an order form from the back of *Rolling Stone* magazine, I became an ordained minister in the Universal Life Church specifically to officiate at their wedding. A belief in God was not required, but the $10.00 admin fee was mandatory.

"Kelly was having some drinks with Eris last night," Bill continues. "They got pretty hammered, and Eris made an ... um ... confession of sorts."

Shit.

"She made Kelly swear to secrecy, but now Kelly's really freaked-out and doesn't know what to do."

I understand the subtext: Eris dropped a hundred-pound dung sack on Kelly, who dropped it on Bill, who now wants to drop it on me.

"Ok. Let's have it," I say.

"Eris is having an affair."

It's a larger dung sack than I am prepared for, and I almost buckle under the weight. A ball expands in my throat cutting off my ability to speak or breathe.

"I know," says Bill. "It's pretty fucked up. I thought you should know. What are you going to do?"

The load crushes me into the parking lot asphalt. I think of my brother, my tiny nephew, even my wayward sister-in-law. Regardless of any action I take, no one will walk away unscarred.

"I don't know." I move slowly toward the motel room door. "I don't know."

The news of the single's implosion darkens the van despite the bright California sunshine beaming through windows. I lay on the bench seat studying the hundreds of bumper stickers that line the ceiling. Bands, clubs, radio stations and random bits of store-bought wit cover the metal from windshield to rear window, mementos of countless shows, cities, and truck stops. I push aside thoughts of the record and wonder how Mia is doing in her new job.

"*It could happen to you,*" says The Gnome. I ignore him. "*It starts innocently enough. A guy asks a few questions about a stupid Land Rover no one wants, which casually segues into witty banter and a little innocent flirtation.*"

I pay no attention.

"*He judges his timing carefully, waiting for just the right laugh, then slips in a 'Hey, I'll be at the bar later, drop by and I'll buy you a drink.'*"

I roll my eyes.

"*Later, after a hard day, she's thinking she could use that drink, and drops in to see if the charming gentlemen is there ... Oh, there he is! The drinks flow, the laughter gets louder; subtle gestures are exchanged, a hand on an arm, a stray hair brushed from a face ... Someone suggests they move*" *the party upstairs, and that's it! Your girl is doing the Saddle Straddle all night long with Mr. Massengill."*

I still ignore him.

"Yeah," says The Gnome, *"It's an impossible scenario, even though she's hotter than a blast furnace—if you don't mind my saying so. But you're right. I'm sure she adheres to the same bizarre monogamy fixation you cling to. It's perfectly normal. Who would want to have exciting sex in a far-off city with a charming stranger, especially if no one would ever have to know?"*

"When we get home, I am going to pulverize you with a hammer and sprinkle the powdery remains in my neighbor's dog food. The next time I see you I'll be shoveling dog shit off my lawn."

The Gnome laughs, long and hard. *"Hey buddy, no hard feelings,"* he says. *"Besides, why would she cheat on you when all this success is raining down around here? You got your big hit song that just ate shit with a soup spoon, despite all the rock star BS you keep feeding her. That Ferrari is beginning to look a lot like a used Hyundai."*

"Yeah, that reminds me," I reply, "I thought you were supposed to be our good luck charm? What the fuck? It's been nothing but a dumpster fire since the moment you got here."

"Dude," says The Gnome, *"you really need to brush up on your little people mythology. Leprechauns have the pot of gold. Do you see a shillelagh around here? A four-leaf clover? No. I am a Gnome, born in the land that brought you The Black Plague, Vikings, two World Wars, and Nazis. We travel around underground, and for some inexplicable reason, pointlessly loiter on suburban lawns."* He paused. *"God, I hate your stupid lawns ... But does any of that sound lucky to you?"*

The longest stretch of any tour is the last five miles before your house. The van shrinks. The Funk smells worse. The anticipation of your own bed, homecoming sex, and food prepared by someone other than a pimple-faced teenager with a deep fryer, slows the van to a barely discernable crawl. You stare out the windshield fixated, familiar landmarks rolling by, while gasoline and willpower close the gap between yourself and the one place for which your entire being yearns: home.

Today, I am going to ruin that experience for my brother. In the back of the van, along with his suitcase and guitar, is a gigantic dung sack with which I have to burden him, decimating the glorious ritual of homecoming.

The van rolls up to JT's house. He pops open the door and says his goodbyes, when I inject "Hey, can I talk to you?" as we step out onto the driveway.

There are no words, gestures or tonalities that cushion a statement like "I have been told that your wife is having an affair." The suck is so fully entrenched in every syllable that it simply cannot be extracted, nor glossed, nor spun in any kind of positive light. So, I just let him have it, both barrels, right to the heart.

He has questions I cannot answer and pain I cannot begin to alleviate. He stares blankly at his front door as my ineffectual attempts at comfort spill out in an awkward stream of irrelevance, each word coming slower, until the last one just falls to the driveway.

"Well, I guess that's it. Thanks Bro," he says giving me a hug. "Are you okay?" he asks me.

"Jesus Bro, don't worry about me..." I crawl back into the van and slouch into the seat, wiping an eye on my shirt sleeve. Through the window I see my brother immobilized in his driveway, staring at his front door.

No one says a word, not even The Gnome.

Later that evening I'm home too, but the apartment is empty. Mia is in Chicago or Philadelphia or New York or somewhere. Ashlei is staying with relatives 100 miles away. I open a window to expel the stale, month-old atmosphere, then poke around at the rotting vegetables and rancid milk in the fridge. I doubt Dorothy would click her ruby slippers for this.

The light is flashing on the answering machine.

"He baby, it's me," says Mia through the tiny speaker. "I thought you would be home by now. I hope your drive went smoothly. It's late here, like 2 a.m., so I'm going to bed. We'll talk tomorrow ok? I love you."

I rewind the message and listen to it again, reading between the lines, mining as much non-verbal information as I possibly can: the tone of her voice, her inflection on certain syllables. When it's over I rewind just enough to hear the last three words.

I do it again, and again, and again.

When I turned 30, I treated myself to a small existential meltdown. To me, 30 was the demarcation line between kid and adult. Up until this point I had an easy excuse for all shortcomings, failures, and stupid mistakes: *I'm just a kid*. On the other side of this line was: *What the hell is wrong with you? Why can't you get your shit together?*

Prior to 30, I had one simple goal, Total World Domination, and boy, was I going to get around to that pretty soon. But after blowing out 30 candles, a troubling thought swirled in my oxygen-deprived brain: total World Domination may require effort.

Within a few weeks of the traumatic passing of my third decade all these thoughts congealed into a song called "Is That Me." Originally the lyric had a line, "Could it be I lived these 30 years," but when I brought the song to the band Bill made me change it.

"Dude," he had said shaking his head, "there's no such thing as a 30-year-old in a rock band."

Bill was the self-appointed Cool Police in The Uninvited. Begrudgingly we went with it based on qualifications like coolest hair, not to mention he sported a goatee long before the Seattle Chin Fuzz Explosion. Consequentially, with a simple "Are you really going to wear that?" Bill could send you running for the dressing room moments before stepping out on stage.

Following the demise of "What God Said," no one had any idea whether or not Atlantic would be willing to release another single. Though my insides were a bubbling cauldron of panic, self-doubt, and paranoia, whatever fortitude I had left insisted on a constant façade of Everything Is Fine. It was a system of internal disaster management I cultivated for years. Some would call it denial, unhealthy and unrealistic, but for me denial is a workable solution.

I presented my Everything Is Fine argument to the band backed with no evidence other than simply denying that everything was turning to shit. Fortunately, my brother is equipped with many of the same coping mechanisms. He bought into my *"Let's put blinders on and pretend that none of this is happening"* argument without question, which cascaded over the rest of the band like a waterfall of irrationality. Unified in unfounded optimism, we decided our record deal was not dead.

But if another shot was forthcoming, we wanted that song to be "Is That Me" in hopes of showing a deeper, more reflective side of the band. We called everyone associated in anyway with the label, applying equal parts charm and irritant, hoping to sway our autocratic media overlords.

It worked, but only halfway. Atlantic would release another single, but that song would be "Too High for the Supermarket." We were skeptical about releasing another "funny" song. The road to Irrelevance is paved with novelty tunes. But Atlantic pointed out that "Too High" was already getting play on morning shows around the country. By all indications it could blossom into the Stoner Anthem of Our Time. A lofty goal, but hey, reach for the stars, right? Furthermore, the record company was backing its argument with the promise of tour and marketing support and the unmentioned, yet fully understood, postponement of our ejection back into the Abys of the Unsigned. You can't fill the tank with artistic integrity, so we cave to the wishes of the label.

JT was dented. The emotional abrasions were evident around the corners of his smile, but the smile existed, nonetheless. His easy confidence had an air of resignation as he threw his gear into the back of the trailer. Several days earlier Eris had left with his son, back to her parents in Nebraska.

"You okay?" asked Bruce closing up the trailer.

"I am more than okay," replied JT. "Today, I start Life 2.0. And to celebrate, this tour is going to be a coast-to-coast Bloosh-Fest." Eyebrows rise as heads turn inquisitively towards my brother. "That's right," JT continues, "I will be having sex with pretty much anyone who wants it, and standards will be lowered to accommodate all comers, so to speak. I am now a single guy playing in a rock band and I intend to behave like one."

We all laugh as we pile in the van, but Tony and I share a quick look of apprehension.

The first show is in Las Vegas, which dampens the usual high spirits at the beginning of a tour. Vegas itself is fine but rolling out of the Bay Area a certain "can't-get-there-from-here" feeling permeates. No direct route exists. God, in an obvious effort to aggravate traveling rock bands, placed a gigantic mountain range between Northern California and the rest of the United States. Consequently, we have to drive all the way to LA, then head north again to Vegas, forming an ironic 600 mile smile on the map. The geographic bummer also applies to travelers going in the other direction. History buffs may recall the Donner Party ran into the same obstacle during the Gold Rush, having a major impact on meal planning among other things.

This morning I claim the driver's seat in an effort to stave off the agonizing monotony of Highway 5. I like tomatoes as much as anyone else but after a couple hundred miles they lose their allure. Long, straight, flat, and black, the road bisects the landscape, disappearing into the horizon. Though LA is about 400 miles away you can almost see it way down there at the end, never getting closer no matter how fast you drive.

The speedometer says 80 miles-per-hour, but we might as well be parked given the lack of change in scenery. How many tomatoes can one country eat? In the back of my mind I hear The Gnome babbling something about JT *"Living the dream,"* which reminds me of a recurring dream I had again last night.

I'm on stage with a band of rock legends in front of a screaming stadium crowd. Eric Clapton is standing right next to me tearing the ass out of his Stratocaster on a solo that has the audience in euphoric hysteria. For three full minutes he keeps the crowd on the edge of climax, teasing them with his uncanny virtuosity. Finally, he hits the crescendo on a tension building full-step bend around the 23rd fret, milking the vibrato for a perfect 4-bar sustain, then turns to me and says, "Take it man!"

Fuck you Eric Clapton.

After three hours of driving, tomatoes give way to the massive feedlot in Coalinga where thousands of cattle stand packed together knee deep in their own shit. It was this very feedlot and its unforgettable stench that inspired author Michael Pollan to write *The Omnivore's Dilemma*, the renowned treatise on modern-day factory farming. The sight and smell turn every member of the band into vegetarians, right up until we reach Kettleman City fifteen minutes later where an In 'n Out Burger induces carnivorous amnesia. Hedonism drowns compassion in ketchup and melted cheese.

We wash down any lingering guilt with the last few swallows of chocolate shake and resign ourselves to three more hours of monotony until Los Angeles. Mercifully, we avoid the city itself and cut across the top of LA County, driving east then north again into the Mojave. The desert's wild beauty is a welcome reprieve from the industrial greenery of Highway 5.

In the time it takes for a charcoal briquet to become a diamond we pass the final landmark before the Nevada border: Bun Boy, Home of the World's Biggest Thermometer. Though the name of the place is steeped in a homo-eroticism that we would rather not contemplate, the World's Biggest Thermometer is pretty damn exciting when your last big thrill was a left turn at Bakersfield. We cheer, then argue again about how many gallons of mercury it would take to fill the World's Biggest Thermometer. The discussion of the environmental impact of spilling all that mercury lasts all the way to the famous "Welcome to Fabulous Las Vegas" sign.

Our first destination is a Vegas radio station where we will be doing an acoustic version of "Too High."

In-studio performances are a bit of a mind-fuck. Most of the time the band is crammed into a tiny booth with a glass window where the DJ smiles back at you over a ginormous microphone. Though he appears to be your only audience member, you are well aware that out there in the ether, thousands of listeners are going about their lives, driving cars, doing dishes, maybe falling in love, maybe crushing someone's heart. Regardless, your insignificant acoustic performance is potentially being heard by more people than any other gig you've ever played in your entire life. But you will never know. The applause, enthusiastic or lackluster, does not exist.

About 20 miles outside of Las Vegas we tune into the station. That's when it happens. As Bare Naked Ladies' "One Week" fades out an unmistakable driving bass line comes pounding through the speakers: Bill's intro to "Too High". Everyone snaps bolt upright straining against seat belts to lean in toward the radio.

"Turn that shit UP!" exclaims JT, cranking the volume knob from the passenger seat.

Bruce's syncopated backbeat comes hammering in and suddenly everyone in the band is a drummer, pounding the air with imaginary sticks.

Nothing, not even sex, feels as good as hearing your song on the radio for the first time.

Imagine you had a bad day. Let's say you went home after the shit storm, sank into your couch and reached for your guitar. You strum a few chords, syphoning off a little of the day's suck. A melody floats to the top so you start humming. The anxiety, stress, and injustice reduce down into a few lines until slowly, miraculously, a song is born unto the world. Maybe you take that song to your best friends. Maybe they hear something, add a little of their own juju, make the song bigger and juicier than you ever imagined.

It is impossible to describe the feeling of hearing that song on the radio, knowing that countless strangers, at that very moment, are indefinably connected to you and some long forgotten shitty day. For three and a half minutes you share a sliver of your life with the whole world, and that one bad day, the crappy day that started it all, becomes *the best day* of your entire life.

That night we play the House of Blues in Vegas, sharing the bill with the inexhaustible Young Dubliners. During the set I notice that JT is making a lot more eye contact with the first few rows than usual. He has his omnipresent smile, but unseen machinations are going on behind those probing eyes.

He's hunting.

The songs have become so much a part of my muscle memory I don't have to give much thought to playing or singing, which is a good thing as I am fascinated by the subtle mating ritual unfolding next to me. JT has found his quarry. No longer scanning the crowd my brother has locked onto a tall brunette on the dance floor, young and uninhibited in her movement. He is singing directly at her. The rest of the audience has been dismissed. He is literally drilling this girl with lyrics, rhythmically pumping the syllables. All the while Ms. Brunette has locked onto his gaze, eyes wide like a Japanese anime cartoon, her body responding to the auditory thrusting.

Good god. I turn away. It's like watching a family member's homemade porn.

After the show I see the two of them at the bar as the Young Dubliners do their thing. He is apparently telling the world's most interesting story because she is enraptured, sipping her drink, looking up at him with full moon eyes while running her thumb and forefinger up and down the length of her straw. Needless to say, JT doesn't make it back to the hotel.

The next morning we are all waiting in the lobby when a yellow taxi pulls up and pours out my brother. He arcs toward the door at a 15 degree angle, struggles visibly with the handle, then finally notices the "Push" sign. He stumbles in with a rush of hot desert air and the smell of semi-digested alcohol.

"You ok? How did it go?" I ask.

"I'm not really sure," he says. "The night is a bit fuzzy, but I can say that things were a little awkward this morning. She was kind of upset to wake up in a vomit lake. She blamed me but I clearly saw a French fry in there, and I haven't had those in weeks."

"Did you get her number?"

"Nope."

"What's her name?"

"Already forgotten."

"Ok. Let's blow this pop shop."

Tony had a laptop, a rare extravagance for a person in our income bracket. He carried 100 feet of telephone cable everywhere we went, and snaked it all over the hotel rooms, restaurants or truck stops, plugging into any available phone jack in order to steal a few minutes on his AOL account. Sitting at a diner I stare at the grey cable running along the countertop and disappearing into the back kitchen, its access paid for with a CD, a t-shirt, and a five-dollar-bill.

Tony's eyebrows fold together as he studies the screen. "Guys, I have some good news that I think is actually bad news, but it's still pretty cool, but may suck really hard."

Bill takes a pull from his coffee and sets it down on the counter. "Great. I could use a lift that will bum me out at the same time."

"Have you guys heard of Napster?" asks Tony.

We all had some knowledge of the free file sharing platform used primarily by teenagers to swap MP3 music files. From what I understood Napster's business model was to make money by convincing wealthy investors that what they were doing was so cool and cutting edge it would eventually make money by just existing. Because it was on the Internet. And it was cool. So money would just materialize. My inner communist loved the idea. Not only were they sticking it to The Man they were making music more accessible to everyone.

"If I'm seeing this correctly," said Tony, "songs from The Uninvited have been shared over five-hundred thousand times!"

"Holy shit that's incredible!" says Bruce.

"Maybe," says Tony, "But it's also bad. Think about it. Who would buy a record if they could get the songs for free? If those file shares had been sales, we would have a gold album right now."

My inner capitalist picks up a briefcase stuffed with hundred-dollar bills and beats my inner communist to death. "A gold album! Jesus, we would have a bus, a crew, real food..." I pour out my spoonful of runny oatmeal.

"We're not the only ones," says Tony looking at the screen.

"Bon Jovi, Metallica, Third Eye Blind ... everyone is on this thing."

"At least our name is getting out there," says Bruce, "It might help ticket sales."

"It might," says JT, "but I have a bad feeling about this. In the immortal words of David Bowie, 'Ch-ch-ch-changes, turn and face the strain.'"

For the next few days I couldn't stop thinking about Napster. Apparently, it was on the minds of several record companies too. After all, if the major labels are kicking down several hundred thousand dollars for recording and marketing an album, they're hoping for more return than a thumbs-up emoji from an 11-year-old playing on his mom's computer.

In hopes of shutting down the fire hose of freebees, A&M Records was suing Napster for copyright infringement. I had not fully decided whether that was a good thing, but I did know for certain that the situation was a lot like pulling out an 8-ball of cocaine in front of a bunch of bored housewives at an 80's Tupperware party. That shit is not going back in the bag.

Having procured the usual array of potato chips, tiny chocolate donuts, Milky Way bars, and diet sodas—gotta watch that waistline—we wait outside a dusty 7-Eleven on the outskirts of Phoenix while JT finishes up in the phone booth.

"I just spoke with Braveheart," he says strolling back. "Our radio play is awesome in Phoenix, but another Atlantic artist is burning up in Detroit and stealing our thunder. Everyone at the label is excited about this guy while we are slowly slipping into ugly stepchild territory."

"Who's the artist?" asks Bruce.

"Some dude who calls himself 'Kid Rock,'" says JT.

"What kind of poser calls himself Kid Rock?" says Bill.

"The kind that has a number one song in Detroit," says JT. "But here's the deal: if we sell more copies in Phoenix then this jag wagon sells in Detroit, Atlantic's love light will shine upon us once more."

"How can we *not* outsell a guy who calls himself Kid Rock?" says Bill.

"Agreed," says JT. "But I think we need an insurance policy. I propose we dip into the band fund and drive around Phoenix all day buying up every single copy of our CD in every single record store in this town."

"That could be hundreds of CDs costing thousands of dollars," says Our Man Tony. "If we don't make that money back it will jeopardize the rest of the tour and maybe the next."

"That's right," says JT, "but if this single flops then the album is done anyway. No band gets a third single if the first two bite the dust."

"I'll put my own money in," says Bill.

"So will I," says Bruce.

We all agree. After everything we have been through this isn't the time for pussification. Like five General Custers, we pile into the van and drive straight into the heart of Phoenix.

While T-Money plots a course to every record retailer in town, I start digging through the van's CD collection. Every week, in whatever town we are playing, the local Atlantic rep gives us the new releases. It's astonishing the amount of music one record company produces in a single week. Most of it is dreck wrapped in shinny production; you can hear the money but not the soul. Some of it is pure stunning genius, but that particular quality has nothing to do with whether or not the record is a hit. Either flavor is equally subject to the whims of the evil bitch goddess, Lady Luck.

Thumbing through spines I find the CD I'm looking for,

Devil Without a Cause by Kid Rock. On the cover is a sticker for radio people saying, "Featuring 'Cowboy.'" I put on my headphones, slide the disc into my Sony Discman and hit the "Play" button. The harmonica and guitar intro fire up, and I feel my lips purse just a touch. The backbeat starts and my head bobs involuntarily while my index finger picks up the groove on my thigh.

Damnit. It doesn't suck.

Then the rap verse starts in. My head tilts about five degrees to the right. I let four full lines flow through my audio processors but no reference material is forthcoming. This is some different shit.

"This is some different shit," echoes The Gnome.

Interestingly, "Too High" also has a kind of rap feel, I think to myself.

The Gnome chimes in, *"'Too High' is whiter than white-boy rap. It's like French Vanilla with marshmallows left in a snowbank. Comparing your song with this is like comparing KC and The Sunshine Band to Doctor Dre."*

It has a novelty aspect like "Too High," I reply.

"Yeah, right," says The Gnome. *"He's talking about going to Hollywood to fuck countless hookers while you guys are talking about being so stoned you can't follow a two-item grocery list. There's cool novelty and there's dork novelty. A song that ponders the birthplace of radicchio, well, you tell me which category that falls into."*

The Gnome has a point, and it depresses the hell out of me.

"You should talk to Mia," he says then. *"That will make you feel better. How long has it been anyway? Five days? A week? I wonder what's going on there? Isn't she in the Midwest somewhere? Maybe she hooked up with this Kid Rock guy. Sounds like he's going places..."*

I glance over at The Gnome with his permanent cherub smile set in plaster. "Tony," I say, "can you do me a favor and chuck that thing out the window?"

"I thought he was a good luck charm?" comments Tony,

studying a map. "I think we need all the luck we can get right now."

Twenty minutes later we pull into Tower Records for our first CD purging. Wasting no time I navigate quickly through the rock isles looking for the "U" section, then flip through the titles in alphabetical order. There, between "Uncle Tupelo" and "U2," is the bin marker for "The Uninvited." There's one CD left.

I grab the disc and stare for a moment at the familiar cover. Here is our music, in a store, in a town, in a state, where I don't know anyone, yet anyone who picks this up knows a part of me. Weird. I take the CD to the cashier and ask the punker chick behind the counter if they have any more in stock. She checks her computer and shakes her mohawk. This is the last one.

Next on the list is Warehouse Records but they are sold out. We venture into the mall to hit Sam Goody, but they are cleaned out too. The same goes for all the rest of the Tower locations and every independent record store in the greater Phoenix/Tempe metropolitan area.

After 12 hours we call off the search, having procured a grand total of one CD.

"One whole sale," says The Gnome. *"Boy, that's gonna light up the charts! They'll be popping the champagne up at corporate for sure!"*

Confused and slightly dejected, we head back to the motel wondering what the hell is going on. Who's in charge of stocking? It doesn't take a Harvard MBA to figure out that sales quotas will be negatively impacted if there's nothing to buy.

The motel is in a shady part of town. Gang graffiti is scrawled all over dilapidated liquor stores and various abandoned commercial buildings. In situations like this, one of us sleeps in the van to protect the irreplaceable equipment, but I always thought the policy was somewhat flawed. Is an emaciated musician really a viable deterrent, or in the event of an actual break-in would our net losses include a band member beaten to death with a tire iron?

I draw the short straw and end up in the van. Laying in my sleeping bag on the bench seat I quietly rehearse my surrender speech in preparation for the crash of a broken window.

Eventually my thoughts turn to Mia and our inability to connect via pay phone. I resolve to bite the financial bullet and use the cell phone tomorrow. But the undercurrent to all this is the situation with the lack of CDs in the stores. Is this a chronic issue across the country, or is it a good thing that the stores are empty?

Mercifully, sleep finally descends accompanied by distant sirens, traffic noise, and The Gnome softly humming the chorus to "Cowboy."

"Do you know what a 'gusher' is?" asks JT.

"Unless we are talking about slang terms used in the 19th century oil boom, I can't say that I do," I answer.

JT had just wandered into the I-HOP where we sit poking at a plate of pancakes the size and flavor of a stack of Frisbees. Last night he disappeared after the show at Liquid Joes in Salt Lake City. He never made it back to the motel, but that was standard operating procedure these days.

"Ok," says Bruce, "what's a 'gusher'?"

"I don't want to put you off your pancakes," says JT, settling into a chair and grabbing my coffee with an expression of askance.

"I don't think there's anything that can make these pancakes less appetizing," I say, "Please, enlighten us."

"I had never heard the expression either," JT began, "But this girl I was with..."

"What was her name?" I interrupt.

"It's been blotted from my memory by Post-traumatic Stress Disorder," says JT. "Anyway, I'm a giver, and I like to make sure that a girl I'm with is having a good time, so you know, I'm on my way downtown when she says, 'Just so you know, I'm a gusher.' Well, that didn't really mean anything to me, and I wasn't in a frame of mind to be processing potential red flags, so I just get to work, you know?"

Bill pushes the plate of pancakes to the far end of the table.

"So," continues JT, "the moment of truth is dawning, if you know what I mean, when suddenly I'm taking it in the face like a firehose."

A jet of tepid coffee sprays violently from my nose. Everyone pushes back from the table, swearing and blotting coffee from their t-shirts, but no napkin ever created can wipe clean the indelible stain JT placed in our minds.

"Ok then," interjects Tony, "I think we can safely assume that this concludes breakfast. We got a schedule to keep so let's get out of here."

Later that day we make some calls to Atlantic to get the low down on why there are no records in the stores. It must be a big day for long lunches because no one is in at the record company. Having exhausted our tiny rolodex we turn to Arthur Spivak who says he'll make some calls. About an hour later we get the word: the reason that stores are not being restocked is because he and Tori have partial ownership of the band's contract, meaning Arthur and Tori get a piece of the pie. On the other hand, Kid Rock is 100% bona fide Atlantic Records with no strings attached so Atlantic makes more money if Rock's record is a hit then they do if ours takes off. Thus, all things being equal, Kid Rock is going to get more company resources if "Cowboy" is looking good in a few markets.

The news casts a shadow over the van. I struggle to find a positive side to help lift the spirits of my comrades, but no matter which way you look at this glass there is no way to see it half-full.

No, this glass is fucking empty—completely, totally, 100% void of liquid of any kind.

Sometimes, you just embrace the suck.

No one wants to drive in Manhattan. Piloting a van and trailer through the slow-churning chaotic vortex of New York traffic is a blood pressure spike we all want to avoid.

Bill gets us over the Brooklyn Bridge, stops at the first red light, and dives out of the driver's seat into the back of the van. "No way," he says, leaving the driver's seat empty and horns blaring behind us.

Tony reluctantly crawls behind the wheel mumbling, "You guys don't pay me enough for this shit."

"We pay you?" asks Bruce.

Everyone is a little on edge, but I am excited to be in the city. Tonight we play one of my favorite NY venues, Brownies, but more importantly Mia is meeting us here. I haven't seen her in eight weeks, the longest we have ever been apart since I first wedged myself into her life, and the anticipation is killing me.

"Can't wait to see her, huh?" taunts The Gnome. *"That's great, but you know, a lot of things can happen in eight weeks. People change, situations change. As the old saying goes, 'Absence makes the heart grow ... in a completely different direction totally dismissing irrelevant past attachments' ... or something like that, you get the point."*

Whatever. The thought of her pressed up against me obliterates any downer espoused by a pointless hunk of semi-decorative stoneware.

One hour and three coronary events later we arrive at our friend Josh's apartment. Josh, whose relationship with the band stems from our earliest days, is attending Rabbinical school after having seen God at a Grateful Dead show in San Francisco two years earlier. I never learned the details surrounding his Divine

Sighting. Was God literally at the show? Did He have a ticket, or did He need a miracle—wouldn't that be the ultimate irony? Was He selling grilled cheese in the parking lot? About 90% of the attendees of a Grateful Dead concert sport flowing grey hair and navel-length beards, a solid Old Testament look. How can one be sure they are actually seeing God and not just Jerry Garcia? Or maybe it's the same thing?

Josh greets us with hugs and smiles at the door, his shorn dreadlocks replaced by a yarmulke. The tiny studio apartment is packed with our East Coast friends including our old roadie, Ninja Bob, but a quick scan of the room reveals that Mia is not there. Our communication has been sparse, mostly through voicemail, but the plan was for her to meet us at Josh's.

I swallow down hard on my disappointment while the happy group around me swaps stories and bong-hits. Josh is less than orthodox when it comes to herb, aligning somewhat with the Rastafarians when it comes to that particular sacrament.

I settle onto the couch and fight back an ominous feeling. Did she seem a bit distant in her last few messages? It's possible she missed her flight, or couldn't get a cab, or accidentally slept in...

Or didn't want to come.

The realization is so heavy I sink further into the couch cushions. Something is wrong. I feel it in a dark corner of my heart. I can't define its source or cause, but the feeling of dread is starting to swell. I have her schedule somewhere in my suitcase. Where was she last? Miami? I'll need to talk to the guys, but I can probably fly out tomorrow. It won't be too hard to find her. We'll have to cancel the show in DC, but who cares.

A light tapping at the door interrupts the conversation; I know that knock. Instinctively I know I have held the hand that produces that sound. Josh opens the door and Mia steps in, almost the exact same way she stepped into the Central years earlier. She floats by Josh with a light kiss before jumping into my arms, and I plant a kiss on her V-Day WWII style. Some small portion of my mind notes that the make-out session may be a bit awkward for others in the close quarters of the studio apartment, so with a quick "excuse us" I pull her into the bathroom.

Pulling off each other's clothes with exclamations of "oh-my-god-I-missed-you-so-much" we dive into serious reunion sex, heedless of the packed room of people six inches away on the other side of the bathroom door. It's cramped and uncomfortable with hard surfaces and sharp corners, but for me it's as good as the Ritz Carlton.

We emerge a few moments later, flushed and breathless, my shirt on inside-out. Her arms wrapped tightly around my waist. We join the party in earnest basking in the warmth of our extended band family. As we laugh and smoke and drink, I make a solemn vow to myself: I will never doubt her again. And more importantly, I will never, ever, allow us to be apart for this length of time again.

That night the show at Brownies rocks. With Mia on the dancefloor, thoughts of Atlantic, CD sales, and music business bullshit are pushed aside, replaced by the love of playing that started it all. After the set Tony mentions that Joan Osborne, who recently had a big hit with "One of us," was in the audience.

JT wades into the crowd to find her and I smile to myself, wondering if she will become an unwitting participant in the Coast-to-Coast Bloosh Fest. That would be amazing. In the first line of Osborne's hit song she sings, "What if God was one of us?" If she woke up with JT, he could introduce her to Josh which could spark quite a theological discussion. What if God was one of us and He also happened to be a fan of the Grateful Dead?

Sadly, the ecumenical repartee was not to be. JT got sidetracked by a small group of catalogue models who wandered into the club after a shoot. They were all drinking Irish Blowjobs or some other nasty concoction that left a green film all over their chins. The last thing I saw as Mia and I were leaving the club was JT, hands behind his back, going down on a shot glass topped with a green, six-inch cone of whip cream while the girls chanted, "CLOV-ER, CLOV-ER, CLOV-ER!"

Later that night, back at the hotel, I tell Mia the whole story about what is going on with Atlantic including Napster, the CD stocking issue, this guy called Kid Rock, everything. She listens intently and understands the ramifications: our three-year odyssey in the corporate media world may be coming to an end. Before I can tell her I have no idea what to do next, the door lock slides open and in walks JT. The price of a night in a New York City hotel room, even a dump like this, is more than a month of rent back home so we are all bunking up together nice and cozy.

JT falls backward on the bed next to us, smelling like Bailey's Irish Cream and Chanel No. 5. "It's over," he says. "Thank God it's finally over."

"What's over?" asks Mia.

"My foyer into junior rock star sexual excess, the Coast-to-Coast Bloosh-Fest. We are officially on the East Coast now so I can knock this shit off."

"Really?" says Mia, laughing. "You're living the fantasy of every adolescent male on the planet and now you want to stop?"

"This may come as a surprise," says JT staring up at the ceiling, "but girls who will have sex with a guy 30 minutes after meeting him, based solely on the fact that he was on stage holding a guitar, usually have a few issues. So many, in fact, they can turn even the most potentially erotic situation into a mundane chore, like washing dishes." He turns his head to face us. "You guys are lucky. Don't fuck it up."

The after-party winds down to the sound of the band and friends lightly snoring in the darkened hotel room. With Mia's head on my shoulder, I feel connected yet lost at the same time. I push back hard on the disappointment surrounding the album's inability to take off, but it seeps in around the edges. We had everything wrapped up tight with a pretty red bow, but somehow, it's all falling through the bottom. It feels vaguely like mourning, but just before I drift off to sleep, I feel Mia's lips on my cheek and her breath in my ear:

"It's ok, everything will be fine."

The hammer fell in Texas. I don't remember the town, maybe Austin, maybe Dallas, but I do remember it was laundry day— crappy news delivered in a crappy laundromat.

"I just spoke with Braveheart," says JT. "It's done. Atlantic pulled the plug on 'Too High' and dropped us. We are officially an unsigned band again. Also, both Braveheart and Spivak are jumping ship, despite their 'undying faith in the project'. They wish us 'The best of luck, blah blah blah ... Eat a dick ...We're done.'"

"Braveheart too? After everything we put up with, he's bailing on us?"

"At least we'll never look at another plate of haggis," says JT.

I once saw a photo of the fall of Saigon in the last days of the Vietnam War. A few lucky soldiers clung to a ladder extending from the bottom of a rising helicopter, leaving hundreds of desperate people below, arms stretched in a hopeless effort to grasp the last lifeline. Getting dropped from the label felt like falling off that ladder back into the wretched throng below.

I finish stuffing a wad of rancid t-shirts into an ancient front-loader, thinking that Daniel Boone could have used this very machine to wash his dirty buckskins before dying at the Alamo. I slam the coin feeder into the machine, harder than necessary, and turn to face my brother.

He's grinning.

The sum total of our shared experience makes verbal communication almost superfluous. One look at his face and I know where his head is.

This is not the end.

This is not defeat.

I smile back and say, "Fuck these guys."

"Fuck. These. Guys," repeats my brother.

We have a national following and a host of powerful connections throughout the industry, thanks to the hundreds of thousands of dollars spent by our good friends at our former label, which we don't have to pay back. We can continue to tour and record for as long as we want. Another gold ring is out there somewhere, and now we have a big, fat metal detector to help us find it.

JT and I formulate a strategy to make lightning strike twice. Airplay landed us our first record deal so all we need is another independent album and a little love from our new friends in radio. That new Ferrari isn't gone, it's just on layaway.

JT leaves to break the news to Bill and Bruce, confident that he can frame it in a way that will make them feel stoked to be out from under the tyrannical thumb of our former Corporate Masters. I pull out my acoustic guitar, hop up on a dryer and have a seat to wait out the wash cycle. The spinning dryer creates a hypnotic rhythm, and I strum along to the thumping. As the heat warms my butt, lyrics fall effortlessly from my lips. Four quarters later the dryer and I write what will become the title song to our next album—

"It's All Good."

A couple months later we are back where it all started, 4th Street Recording in Santa Monica. It smells the same, cedar siding mixed with ocean breeze and stale marijuana, but a lot has changed. Jim Wirt has become a successful record producer, garnering gold and platinum records for his work with Incubus and Hoobastank. It was heartbreaking that Jim would not be working with us, but he was used to getting paid now, and that concept was still foreign to The Uninvited.

All my regrets rise into my throat. Jim should have produced the Atlantic record. We should have told everyone steering us away to fuck off, but we were blinded, sitting in high-rise offices sipping cappuccinos with artless asshats. Anxiety rises as I reflect on a series of bad decisions that stifled our career, but I quickly dismiss the thoughts and get my inner shit together. If the Buddha shows up at this point, I'll be trying to record with a couple of broken ribs.

One of the most profound changes at 4th Street is the addition of a spanking new Macintosh computer sitting right next to the 48 channel mixing board. Inside this magic silver box is a tiny recording studio called Pro Tools, thousands of times more powerful than all the analog equipment that surrounds it. Pro Tools is like virtual steroids, Viagra, and cocaine all mixed together; it enhances performance and is very tempting. Bad notes are tuned to perfection, missed beats pushed back into alignment. But in the process, the software can dehumanize the production, leaving the performances sanitized, pasteurized, homogenized, and hermetically sealed in plastic wrap.

CJ, the studio's First Engineer who will be pushing faders on this project, smiles when JT brings in four rolls of two-inch wide recording tape. Since the introduction of the magic box, the massive 24-track recording machine hasn't seen much love. With Pro Tools you can have 1000-tracks without any expensive, cumbersome, tape reels. But for us, nothing beats the rich, warm sound of tape, so this album will be recorded on the technological equivalent of stone tablets.

The Band Fund dictates that we have exactly 10 days to make this record. There will be no sleeping, no multiple entrees, no interrupting phone calls from rock legends, no judgements handed down by A&R guys with Lamborghini footwear, just four guys with wooden instruments telling stories into microphones.

Once again, just like the early days, the tape reels spin, the lava lamp globs, countless vacuum tubes glow inside of mysterious steel boxes, and slowly the music takes shape.

A few days into the project Jim ducks into the studio to say hi. The reunion creates a moment of nostalgia, but so much has changed. We are saddened to hear that he and his wife Kathleen, who was the business side of the studio, split up. From the outside their relationship seemed so complementary, Jim the ultra-hip music producer and Kathleen the sharp, sexy brain keeping the doors open.

Like most divorced men, Jim did not want to linger on the details. All he said was that the term, "It's alright," when spoken in the context of marriage, doesn't necessarily mean what everyone else understands it to mean. Success, it would seem, is oftentimes paid for with failure.

There are other changes: Bill and Bruce, after recording their parts, disappear into the greater Los Angeles sprawl. In the old days, the whole band hunkered down in the studio, hanging on each note, cheering or criticizing, until the last mix rolled off the tape. Now, other interests beckon, and our rhythm section leaves us to our own devices.

On the positive side, the empty studio gives JT and me a rare opportunity: we can do whatever the hell we want. Ideas don't have to be filtered through producers and band members; they are just seized upon to see if they work. We are two kids let loose in a toy store after hours, and we tear into every box we can get our hands on.

Ten days later, with the sun rising over Santa Monica, we emerge from the studio delivering ten new songs into the world, etched with a laser beam into the aluminum surface of a compact disc. The days of cassette tapes, much like pantyhose, have passed and will never be coming back.

The album is weightier, exorcising demons of divorce and disappointment, but overall wrapped in the sardonic humor that made the band popular in the first place. With critical ears we blast the new tunes heading east on Wilshire Blvd, the sun beaming through the windshield and smoothing the lines of sleeplessness. JT smiles as the last song, "Wasted Years," fades out. No words necessary.

It sounds like redemption.

It sounds like a second chance.

Malltopia

Slack-faced, I languish on the edge of retardation awash in the television's electromagnetic radiation. I'm watching "Who Wants to Marry a Millionaire" or "Gilligan's Island" or "Beverly Hills 90120"—it makes no difference because it's all just pop culture morphine, temporarily numbing the prickly thoughts of the day.

I'm aroused from the trance when Mia steps into the room. I see tears welling in her eyes as her lips quiver in unreadable emotion.

"Whoa, Baby, are you okay?" I push myself up and move toward her.

She nods "yes" like everything is perfectly delightful, but the tears start down her cheeks.

Once more I'm baffled by the eternal feminine mystery. How can a person be completely fine and yet totally fucked up at the same time? Estrogen is the biological equivalent of yin and yang.

Experience has shown, in confusing times like these, you can't go too far wrong with a hug. It's comforting to all parties involved and it gives you time to figure out what the hell is going on.

I wrap her in my arms and make some kind of noise I hope sounds soothing, when she produces a thin white piece of plastic. She looks up from the stick and holds it out for me to examine. In the middle is a small window, and inside the window is a bold, blue plus sign. A little slow, possibly due to the TV sedation, I look at her perplexed.

Then it hits me.

Plus is positive. Plus is addition.

I feel tears of my own well up. On the guest list of life Mia and I are henceforth plus one.

It wasn't unexpected, just a tad ... soon. A few months earlier we were playing a festival with the Dave Mathews Band. As I sat behind the stage strumming my guitar, a shiny, aerodynamic road coach floated into the backstage area. It looked like a spaceship on wheels. When the door slid open in a smooth, UFO-like motion, I was surprised by what emerged: children, laughing and running, followed closely by what I assumed was a high-paid nanny. The assumption was based on three things: her youth—too young to have four kids—her clipboard—a sign of professional organization—and a big smile, the kind that says, "I'm not a mom. I'm going to have a day off soon."

It never dawned on me that a family was even a possibility. But watching the little tykes being herded into a dressing room, suddenly I wanted all of it: the bus, the nanny, the clipboard, the kids, and most importantly, the career that would support all those mouths. Bus envy had just grown exponentially. Someone was living a dream bigger than I imagined, and I always prided myself on dreaming to the point of delusion.

When I got home, I told Mia all about it. She chucked her birth control pills the next day. A few weeks later the kid part of the plan was crossed off the list. As for the rest of it, we could probably afford the clipboard, but everything else would require some additional effort.

The van pulls up, the horn honks, the beckoning door slides open. I feel its pull, like gravity, but this morning it's harder than usual to yield to the summons. I rub Mia's still-flat belly and scratch Ashlei under her greying chin. I imagine Ashlei is relieved that I am the only one traveling now. Mia left Land Rover and took a job as a waitress at the Black Diamond Brewery. The dog will be keeping my spot warm on the bed from now on.

The mood in the van is congenial yet trepidatious. The absence of our record deal is palpable, almost like a missing band member, and the wounds are still fresh. Nothing undermines a person's confidence quite like nationwide rejection. It's like walking into a bar with a million women and leaving without a single phone number. But the sting is somewhat mitigated by a sliver of hope.

"Not So Supermodel," the first single from "It's All Good," is charting at several college and commercial radio stations. JT lifted the melody for the song from Mozart, whose genius made him *the* Rockstar of his day. Whether JT borrowed the riff intentionally or not makes no difference. Amadeus is dead, and more importantly, so are his lawyers. Besides, we could use a little genius right now.

Determination fuels the van on this trip. When you get dumped by a girl, you dream of one day meeting her at a party with a supermodel on your arm, preferably finishing up her PhD in Astrophysics at Harvard. What we all want most in life right now is to see Atlantic Records running from the room in tears, heading home to break dishes in a jealous rage.

Fred Flintstone is zip-tied to our front bumper. Six inches tall, Fred peers boldly down the road ahead, plunging into the future at 60 miles-per-hour. Lashed to the back of the van is Fred's best friend and sidekick, Barny Rubble, who views nothing but the past in a perpetual state of leaving.

Fred gets a glimpse of the future, but the price is high. Snow sometimes piles up on his little plushy head, while pebbles and road grime embed into his face. Over time the sun bleached his body and now he looks like a faded ghost of his former brightly colored cartoon self. Barney, on the other hand, is the last to arrive at any destination, but has fared far better than his forward-looking friend. With his back to the elements, Barny is not concerned with the future. His life is one of quiet reflection.

As the van rolls south on the ubiquitous Highway 5, I feel like Fred, and attempt to take a more Barny-like approach by skimming an old newspaper I find stuffed in the pocket behind the driver's seat. Anna Nichole Smith, who rose to international stardom for her uncanny ability to look good without her clothes on, was pulling front-page headlines following the death of her billionaire husband whom she married only one year earlier. Smith claimed that despite the 60-year age difference and the billion-dollar bank account, she married the guy for love, and thus was entitled to the posthumous cash tsunami her senior citizen step-child was so unfairly blocking. I briefly attempt to do the math: what is the hourly rate of a billion-dollar paycheck for 365 days of marriage?

A few pages deeper into the paper, a group of scientists announced that the Human Genome Project, an international research effort to sequence and map all the genes of our species, was nearing completion. Touted as the greatest scientific breakthrough of our time, the HGP promised to change the course of modern medicine, curing everything from cancer to erectile dysfunction, and even altering the path of our own evolution. The positioning of these two stories—celebrity fucktastrophe in front, world changing science in the back—incrementally lowered my confidence in the survivability prospects of our species.

I set down the paper with a long, pathetic sigh, embarrassed that in my own life's work Anna Nichole Smith would be considered more of a colleague than any scientist allaying the roots of human suffering.

"Shut the fuck up," says The Gnome. "First of all, you'll never look as good without your clothes on as Anna Nichole Smith, so don't even try to compare yourself to her in any way. Secondly, you hardly know your way around a fretboard, never mind the human genome, so just forget about all that egg-head bullshit too. You know what you're qualified to do? Ride around aimlessly in a van with four other losers."

Next to the paper is a stack of mail Tony picked up from the PO box before rounding us all up. Most people communicated with the band via email these days, but a few diehards still scribbled notes on paper. Email is efficient, sanitary, environmentally friendly, gluten-free, non-GMO correspondence, but something meaningful exists in a tangible piece of paper manipulated by real human hands.

I grab the first envelope off the stack, tear it open and quickly scan the lines. It's the standard "You guys are great send me some free stuff." These types of requests are fulfilled based on the number of interesting adjectives utilized. "Awesome," "amazing," and "cool" are prominently featured here so this guy gets a signed 8x10 glossy photo.

I continue leisurely through the small stack until one hand-written message, torn from a binder notebook, makes me sit upright. "Guys," I say, "Check this out."

I read the letter aloud:

"Dear Uninvited,

I decided to die today. I won't bother you with the reasons, they have been stacking up my whole life. I found my wasteoid mom's sleeping pills and poured them out in my hand, but your album was playing in the background and I got distracted.

For some reason by the end of the CD I didn't feel much like killing myself anymore. I'm not saying that you saved my life or anything, but you did get me through a really bad day.

I just wanted to say thanks for that, and I hope you guys are doing well."

It wasn't signed, and there was no return address. It may have been real; it may have been a simple case of teen drama but given my own state of mind the ability to change the course of a single day for just one person in the whole world was enough for me at that moment. Perhaps we too were just B-list celebrity fuckastorphes in the making, just maybe not today.

I peek around the corner of the curtain to see how the crowd size is doing, but I wish I hadn't. A handful of people are milling about in the open-air venue whose capacity is over one thousand, looking like lost souls wandering around purgatory. It's the first night of the South by Southwest Music Festival in Austin, TX, an event we have attended every year for the last 10 years.

Back in the early days of the band we would hang out in the lobby of the Four Seasons hotel, pouncing on producers and A&R people trying to relax at the bar, shoving cassette tapes in their faces while imploring them to come out to our showcase 10 miles out of town. Not this time. We were the "buzz band" this year, with the local press talking about our radio play despite the fact that we were unsigned. There would be no milling about the bar like musical hookers. If the record geeks wanted to see us, they knew where to find us.

And they would have plenty of room to dance because this house was empty.

"I don't get it," I say walking into the dressing room. "There is no one here. We got radio, we got press, what gives?"

Without management or a label the band had become its own promotion machine, making calls, mailing CDs, and generally pushing through the "no's" to get to the "yeses". This whole tour was a test to see if our big-boy pants fit.

JT assumes a posture of nonchalance while tuning his guitar. "Don't sweat it, they'll be here." A line between his eyebrows exposes his unease.

No one wants a return to the bad-old-days of playing to the waitresses, but the unspoken possibility hangs in the humid Texas air: Atlantic records left with our mojo.

Regardless of crowd size, show time is show time. I grab a handful of Altoids and chew them quickly, washing down the peppermint thunder with a can of Red Bull and a long pull off a gin 'n tonic. If we are only playing to the waitresses tonight then the staff are going to *remember* this show, godddammit. I can feel the peppermint burning in my tear ducts.

"Ok let's do this shit."

We huddle up side-stage, guitars slung, while the local DJ plugs his station. Finally, our introduction booms through the empty night:

"...Alright Austin, give it up for THE UNINVITED!"

The ensuing roar could not possibly have been created by waitresses, unless a nationwide Servers Convention just happened to be in town. Astonished, we stroll out onto the stage before a magically packed house. How do a thousand people wondrously materialize in a matter of ten minutes?

Who cares. The mystery is dismissed as a wave of euphoric relief washes over me. We are still loved, and I love the love with loving loveliness.

As JT hammers out the introductory riff of "Mega Multi Media Hero" I deliver the opening lines with the power of the knowledge that this will not be the last time I sing this song.

After the show T-Money brings more good news: we sold out our entire stock of CDs and most of our t-shirts, and this is only the first night of the tour. The resulting parade of Benjamins is double what we made at the door, setting our venture on the path to profitability.

As Tony and I make plans to restock in Dallas, JT steps up and shoves a business card in my face. "Brad Dickgobbler from Capitol Records loves him some Uninvited!"

Tony raises his eyebrow in a fit of enthusiasm, the fullest demonstrable extent of T-Money's excitement, but strangely all I feel is a tepid sense of deja vu. This card could be the key to reopen the gates of rock Valhalla, so why wasn't my heart pounding against my ribs to the rhythm of Queen's "We Will Rock You?" Expensive studios, a tour bus, luxurious hotels all awaited behind this little rectangular piece of card stock, nicely embossed with the words "Capitol Records."

Or not. Lurking in the shadows the realm of possibilities also included unbearable disappointment, agonizing disillusionment, emotional road-rash, and the ultimate demise of the band itself. Do we really need to be "discovered" again? It would appear that we had already been discovered a thousand times tonight resulting in a complete sellout of all the CDs we stocked for this entire tour. Maybe there was another path, a smarter path that didn't end in a corporate woodchipper.

I consider banishing Capital Records to the Vault of Impossibility, for safety reasons, but in the end, I just set it by the door surrounded with caution tape and a red chalk outline.

Virginia Beach was cold despite the sun. On the white sand a massive stage and lighting rig dwarfed the small group of festival goers huddling against the front of the barricade, as much for warmth as for entertainment value. The promoter sulked around backstage wondering where all the people were, but a biting wind attracts few bikinis. We hammered out our set with workman-like precision before running off to the local Waffle House for a cup of thin, yet gloriously hot coffee.

Bill dropped the bomb after his first sip—

"Guys, I'm done."

"Done with what?" I asked with a level of obtuseness I later found disturbing.

"Done with touring, done with the band, done with everything. I love you guys, but I just missed my kid's first steps. Also, my wife just gave him his first Taco Bell, a milestone I was hoping to put off another 10 years, but since I'm not there this kind of bullshit is taking place on a daily basis. I have to get home."

We had seen this coming for quite some time but chose to cordon it off behind thick curtains of denial. A week earlier I had found him curled in a ball under a table backstage 10 minutes before a show.

"What the hell, Bill, are you okay?"

"I'm fabulous."

"What are you doing under there?"

"Oh, just lying here hoping you'll stop asking me questions."

"Is there anything I can do for you?"

"You could go away. That would be awesome."

"Ok."

I went back to the van, grabbed the cell phone and dialed his wife. In hopes of keeping the phone bill down below four digits, I forego the customary introductory pleasantries. "Hi Kelly, Bill is curled up in a ball under the deli tray and we kinda need him to, you know, play bass tonight. Could you talk to him?" I walk backstage, reach under the table and hand him the phone. He takes it without looking at me.

"Hi Kelly," he says, assuming correctly that I would use the only bullet available to me. I can't hear Kelly's side of the conversation, but I imagine it sounds like a concerned mom talking a teenager off the ledge of a high-rise.

"Ok fine. I love you too."

Bill rolls out from under the table and brushes past me.

"Showtime," is all he says.

Now, at the Waffle House, Bill's resignation has rendered the table speechless. No phone call to Kelly is going to bandage this rift. A certain serenity in my friend's demeanor makes it clear that a decision has been reached after long internal deliberation.

I open my mouth to let fly the thousands of reasons why he is mistaken, making the wrong decision, throwing away the opportunity of a lifetime, but no words come. Bruce and JT look down at their coffee, obviously feeling the same.

Bill is done with this life. He is, quite simply, unhappy.

Under the surface I am treating myself to a breakdown, having no idea how the band will survive the loss of a founding member, when JT breaks the awkward silence.

"I understand, Bill, and you are making the right decision. Growing up is when we stop complaining and making excuses and start making changes. It's time to grow up, and I respect and support that."

Bill's gratitude is evident in a small smile, and Bruce and I share similar sentiments. Bill mentions he will of course finish out the tour, but what happens after that is a big, fat question mark.

As Bruce, Tony, and Bill get up to leave the restaurant I glance over at JT.

"Shut up," he says, reading my mind before I can get a single word out. "I am so NOT ready to grow up. The creative adult is the child who survived, Bro. Believe me, I am in it until the wheels fly off."

I exhale long and slowly and head for the van with the rest of my beleaguered crew.

One of the last shows we played with Bill was at Lucy's Retired Surfers Bar in Austin, Texas. (Don't bother looking for it today—it's gone the way of Sketchers and Sony's Walkmans).

Earlier in the day, during an outdoor festival, we befriended the guys from Stroke 9 while having a few Lone Star beers backstage. Bill raised Bruce's ire by double dipping in the ranch dressing with a half-eaten baby carrot while carving out a clearly defined three-finger trench through the sauce. He was unapologetically explaining to our drummer that he could just go fuck right off about it when Luke, Stroke 9's lead singer, stepped up to explain diplomatically that several other trays of crudités were available, and thus no hors d'oeuvre-related altercations would be necessary.

With tempers sufficiently cooled JT thanked Luke and struck

up a conversation. He congratulated the front man on the success of their song "Little Black Backpack," which was currently kicking ass all over radio, and invited the band to come out to our show that night at Lucy's. (No record label meant no tour support, so it was not unusual for us to play two or even three gigs in a 24-hour period to keep the van stocked with Altoids and Red Bull).

Deep into our second set at Lucy's, I spot several members of Stroke 9 stepping through the door, a variety of females in tow. JT, ever one to promote musical community, invites the guys up to jam a tune together. A brief huddle on stage reveals that we all know The Clash's "Should I Stay or Should I Go," and that one or more of these guys is completely bombed out of their minds.

The packed house erupts as we rip into the famous opening chords. The blended band is tearing it up when about halfway through the song, as the tune's protagonist ponders for the fiftieth time whether or not he should indeed stay or go, a penis is brandished through the fly of one of our new friends. Rolling through the chords I try to think back on all the thousands of performances I have ever played, wondering if an exposed dick was ever part of the mix. Nope. This is definitely a first.

Interestingly, the audience reaction is nonchalant. The presentation of an on-stage schlong in a crowded bar just doesn't carry the same opprobrium as it did thirty years ago. Arguably, Jim Morrison of the Doors was the first on-stage dick presenter of the modern rock era, having felt the need to add a little something extra to a concert in Florida back in 1969. The incident got him arrested and sentenced to jail time, but the authorities were kind enough to pardon him ... after he died in Paris.

No arrests, or even consternation, was forthcoming tonight.

A girl from the audience, presumably a close friend, stepped up to the stage, tucked the little fella back into his pants, zipped up the fly and gave his crotch a friendly pat before making her way back to the bar. But alas, this was not the last we would see of him. No sooner had his friend procured her drink than it was right back out again, like an extra band member that neither sang nor played. Again, the girl steps right up and deftly tucks it away with just one hand, mindful of the martini in the other. But this time she gives him a look of mild reprimand before melting back into the crowd.

For over a decade I had managed to play countless shows without the appearance of a single penis, but tonight it happened twice and both the crowd and I are nonplused. At the end of the night when settling-up with the bar no one mentions the incident. I am surprised to find, as we pack up the gear, that the show leaves me somber.

As we approach the end of the twentieth century it seems as though Rock's ability to challenge social norms, to shock and rebel, is fading into the past. The time of cultural upheaval driven by Marshal stacks is over, and I feel like I missed the party.

The addition of Ladd on bass injects a fresh perspective on everything. An accomplished player, Ladd was a veteran of the LA club scene but never left the confines of the city. He was a friend of the band when we lived in LA, and Bill's hand-picked replacement. Everything was new to Ladd, the van, the road, and all that goes along with it.

"This is so fucking cool!" he exclaimed looking around the van the first time we picked him up.

I glanced around myself looking to see if I missed something, but all I saw was the same dilapidated metal box we've been rolling around in for the last two hundred thousand miles.

"Oh great," says The Gnome, *"Gomer Pyle just joined the band. Wait until he sees the deluxe cup holders..."*

But Ladd is downright giddy about the prospect of riding in

this thing all the way from Phoenix, AZ to Woodstock, NY, and slowly his smile and upbeat attitude permeates the van, reminding us all that we are not part of The Machine sitting in windowless cubicles or pumping out plastic doodads. No musician ever says they work in a band. Musicians *play* in a band. Ladd's positive influence is a reminder that despite a lack of amenities or financial stability, we are the fortunate ones.

Our first gig in Woodstock is not only our first show together, it's our first rehearsal. In fact, it's the first time we had ever played together, period. A month earlier we sent Ladd all of our CDs with a note saying, "Learn these songs, but not too well since we don't play them like this anymore."

When Bruce counted off that first tune, we had no idea what would happen. Would he suck? Did we make a tragic mistake? Over the last 10 years Bill had created some mighty big bass shoes.

By the end of the first bar of the first song, I knew The Uninvited would not only survive, but flourish. Ladd dug into his bass with the same enthusiasm he dug into everything. As an extra added bonus his stage performance reflected his general Labrador-like excitement.

At 6 feet 3 inches tall with chiseled features and Nordic ancestry, his shoulder-length hair seemed constantly blown by an unfelt wind of its own. For reasons he never made clear, he chose to wear a kilt with boxers hanging out the bottom. The audience was equally enthralled and repulsed every time he put his boot up on a monitor speaker at the front of the stage.

The next day, however, things returned to the shitter. We were scheduled to play an outdoor festival sponsored by WXRK, the biggest alternative rock station in New York. Third Eye Blind, Eve 6, Bush, and a parcel of other scene kings were on the bill attracting a crowd of over 50,000 people. It was the high point of our year, and our booking agent blurred moral, legal, and ethical boundaries to put us on this stage.

We arrive early as Tony checked the route a hundred times and probably didn't sleep at all to insure there would be no career-crushing fuckups. Strolling between the semi-truck trailers and massive road cases I'm filled with a sense of optimism. We're on our third printing of "It's All Good," and judging from the current surroundings, the band is doing alright.

A few hours later we step up side-stage to watch Marcy Playground do their thing beneath the 10-story lighting rig, but about halfway through their first song I feel a hand on my shoulder. Turning around I'm met with Tony's blank expression.

"We have a problem," he says, beckoning me with a nod.

I follow him back through the maze of road cases to the artist tent where we find Ladd stretched out across four folding chairs, eyes closed, a fragrant bucket of vomit keeping the immediate area clear of staff and musicians.

"Hey Ladd, you okay?" I ask.

"I can't do this."

"Do what?" I ask with my usual density.

"Play. I can't play."

"You're sick?" I didn't see him drinking the night before but it's not like I'm his dad. He could have been pounding vodka straight from the bottle and I wouldn't have noticed.

"No. Well, sorta. It's hard to explain. It's just that … I mean … Damn, *that's a lot of people out there.*"

Of course. Ladd never played a room bigger than the Whiskey which holds a few hundred people at most. On top of that he has to follow a national act at the top of their game, playing songs he never got to rehearse, in front of an audience bigger than the population of half the towns we drove through to get here. He has a right to some pre-gig jitters.

"Laddio," I say in my most soothing voice, "it's just butterflies. Small-winged creatures, harmless, fluttering in your stomach … And judging from that bucket I don't think there are any left in there."

"More like bats," he says. "Giant vampire bats. With chainsaws. Look, I don't want to let you guys down, but," he struggles to his feet, "I have to get some air."

"Should I go after him?" asks Tony.

I shake my head. "He'll be all right," I say, as much for my own benefit as Tony's. In reality I have no idea whether he will be all right or not. No matter which way you look at it a bucket full of vomit is never a good omen.

Fifteen minutes later we are tuning-up side stage, and our new bass player is nowhere to be seen. The crowd roars as the last note of Marcy Playground's "Sex and Candy" rings out, and the band waves goodbye to the audience.

"You better turn up the bass knob on that Marshal," I say to my brother as we walk out on stage, "we might be missing some low-end on this set."

JT shoots me a quizzical look but there is no time to explain as the crew rushes gear on and off all around us. I give my guitar rig a test strum and wonder just how much the show will suck without bass.

"You guys ready," says the stage manager. It's really more of a statement than a question. "Where the hell is Ladd?" asks JT.

"Halfway to the airport," I say, "judging by the way he looked 30 minutes ago."

JT's "oh shit" face lasts about one millisecond before switching over to showtime mode. He gives a nod to the stage manager who cues our introduction.

"All right New York, all the way from San Francisco please make welcome The Uninvited!"

I rip into the guitar intro to "I Shoulda Been an Astronaut." Eight bars into it, when the band is supposed to kick in, I look up and see Ladd execute a flawless Pete Townsend scissor kick and land perfectly on the first beat. Bruce, JT, and I share a grin while Ladd bashes through the chords, running around the stage like a bass-playing Mick Jagger. It seemed impossible that this was the same person who, only moments ago, was completely paralyzed with stage fright.

As usual with shows like this, the one hour set flashes by in a single instant, almost like it never really happened. We leave the stage both exalted and exhausted. Wiping the sweat from my face with the front of my shirt I ask Ladd how he pulled out of his slump.

"Tony gave me some Altoids and Red Bull—soothed my stomach and perked me right up. He also mentioned I would be walking back to LA if I didn't get my ass on stage."

Ladd would have a few more bouts with stage fright as the tour wore on, but never once did it affect his performance. Despite the less than optimal travel conditions, I never heard him utter a single disparaging word.

We had found our new bass player.

At 3 o'clock in the morning, cruising home from the last show of the tour in San Francisco, Bruce unexpectedly blurts out that he too is throwing in the towel.

"Fantastic," says The Gnome. *"The only musician in the band is quitting. But don't worry, I'm sure people will still pay good money to watch the rest of you get arrested for loitering on-stage."*

Having worked his way through two wives Bruce has decided to put some effort into making number three stick. He says he wants to move to Austin and start a new career.

I briefly consider a spiraling decent into self-pity: first Bill and now this bullshit? But it's pointless. As long as the van has tires and people still go to clubs The Uninvited will live on. Sitting in the driver seat I can't see JT in the back, but I know his thoughts as if they were my own: fuck it Bro, tomorrow is a new day.

Eddie, our new drummer, lived in New Orleans. We befriended Eddie while he was working for Cowboy Mouth as a drum tech and side guy. He had a New Orleans jazz cat vibe that somehow increased the cool factor of the band, while his gumbo-infused chops added a sprinkling of *fais do do* to our sound.

We rolled into New Orleans on Saturday morning to pick him up and head over to the House of Blues where we would be opening for the legendary Cheap Trick. Somehow our agent landed us the opening slot which would last for two weeks. Back in high school I wore out two vinyl copies of *Cheap Trick at Budokan,* so I was struggling to tamp down my inner-starstruck post adolescent geek and maintain some semblance of cool.

We grabbed Eddie at his shotgun house just two blocks off Bourbon Street. (It's called a shotgun house because if a was bullet fired through the front door of the narrow home it would exit the backdoor cleanly without striking a wall). Though it is only 10 a.m. Eddie suggests we celebrate the beginning or our new venture with a drink. Pressed for time he directs us to a drive-thru bar that specializes in daiquiris.

"Oh my god what is this place?" says JT as we roll up to the drive-thru window.

"It's a daiquiri joint, man" says Eddie. "Haven't you ever been to a drive-thru?"

"In California we have ... laws. What kind of third-world country allows drinking and driving?"

Slightly perturbed at the swipe at his beloved hometown, Eddie collects the beverages, sealed in Styrofoam cups, from the lady in the window. "We don't allow drinking and driving here," he says as he distributes the frozen concoctions. "As you can see, they gave us five drinks but only four of them have straws. The fifth straw is still sealed in its paper wrapper as it is assumed that the driver will refrain until the vehicle is safely parked."

The drinks themselves are gigantic, hi-octane affairs. Considering that this is my breakfast, I am a drooling, semicoherent mess by the time we arrive at The House of Blues. We head inside to get the lowdown on soundcheck, but I soon find myself wandering aimlessly through the voodoo-themed halls. Upstairs in the dressing room area a guy is leaning against a doorframe, noodling on a guitar. I know that face. A younger, less haggard version of it stared back at me from an album cover for years.

I struggle to gain control of my tongue, which feels like an octopus tentacle coiled in my mouth, while simultaneously trying to figure out a way to present myself as a fellow musician worthy of addressing a multi-platinum Rock God. I close my eyes, take in a gulp of the humid Louisiana air, and summon the Inner Buddha:

Hank Williams' "Jambalaya," plays on an old, scratchy 45 vinyl record. The Buddha and I sit serenely on the edge of the bayou gazing at the Spanish moss and listening to the birds. I have questions, but my octopus tongue is still incapable of forming words. I pick up a small twig so I can write my queries in the mud when an undetected alligator clamps down viciously on my right calf.

"Hello, Robin," I say with only the slightest slur. "My name is Steve and my band, The Uninvited, will be opening for you guys for the next couple weeks. I just wanted to say—I know you get this all the time—but it really means a lot to me to be here and it is truly an honor to be opening for one of my all-time favorite bands." I hold out my hand, a gesture recognized throughout Western World as an invitation to shake and be friends, but he pays it no heed, another gesture recognized the world over as "*fuck off.*"

He doesn't even look at me.

I stand there like a mute idiot with my hand pointlessly extended for an Awkward Eternity before slowly turning and walking away. I had heard the old saying, "Never meet your heroes," but it had never really applied before. Slightly crushed, I wonder sluggishly back downstairs where I find my brother.

"Hey," he says, "I saw you talking to Rick Nielsen! That is so freakin cool!"

Rick? Uh oh.

I called him Robin, as in Robin Zander, the dreamy lead singer to whom Rick plays the clownish sidekick. I probably just kneed his ego right in the sack. What is my major malfunction when it comes to talking to celebrities? Sure, I had just drunk 32 ounces of rum with a splash of daquiri mix while suffering from metaphorical blood loss due to a run in with a spectral alligator, but regardless, when am I going to get my shit together?

I stumble back upstairs to apologize but Rick is gone.

A couple of days later in Athens, Georgia we play an auditorium at UG to a full house. Despite my earlier faux pas I still take every opportunity to go out front and see Cheap Trick after our set. Tonight, I smile broadly as the band launches into "I Want You to Want Me," memories of making out with Bonnie, my high school girlfriend who would later crush me like a sauvignon grape, playing in my head.

Lost in my own world I'm helping out the band with a little air guitar when a voice breaks through my reverie.

"Hey, I caught your set—you guys were great."

"Thank you!" I say still strumming a 1957 Les Paul Goldtop that only I can see.

"You look to be about my age," the guy says. "It must be a trip to open for a band that was so huge when we were kids."

"Oh man," I say, "this is one of the most mind-blowing weeks of my life. It's a live rewind of the soundtrack of my youth, with much better fidelity than my crappy car stereo from back in the day."

Do I know this person? He has a familiar face...

"What are they like in person? Are they cool?"

"I wouldn't know, unfortunately. I managed to alienate Rick

Nielsen with *the very first word* I spoke to him, so we haven't exactly been chumming it up around the pretzel bowl backstage."

"Really? What happened?"

Who is this guy...?

I am about the launch into the story when the slow turning cogs of my brain finally click into place. It's Michael Stipe of R.E.M. I find myself in an odd juxtaposition between old and new with Robin Zander singing in my left ear while Michael Stipe talks in my right. Though I am a fan of R.E.M.—several of their CDs grace the van's music collection—right now I'm just a guy talking to another guy. No summoning of the Inner Buddha will be necessary. I'm not even going to set down my invisible Les Paul.

I give him a brief synopsis of my daquiri addled one-sided exchange with Rick, and he laughs. "I'm Steve by the way," I say holding out a hand that goes thankfully unneglected.

"I'm Michael," he says.

"I really enjoy your music too, Michael."

"Thanks, man."

Wow, can it really be that easy? No drama, no embarrassing slips, no tension, just me chatting with a fellow human being on a balmy night in Athens.

With a friendly nod Michael fades back into the crowd as Rick cuts into his solo on "Surrender." I jam along on my ethereal Goldtop, respectful of the legendary guitarist's note selection, though I do take the liberty of slipping in a few riffs of my own.

The snow begins falling lightly at first. The large furrows on the side of the road indicate that the snowplow had already been through. I imagine from above it must look like God ran his finger through a massive pile of cocaine.

"We should put on chains," I say. "This road will ice up quick."

"Nah," says Ladd with one hand draped over the wheel, "it's just a few flakes, we'll be fine."

"Dude, this isn't California snow, all light and friendly and ready to be molded into jolly snowmen after a day at the beach. This is Colorado snow—the real deal. They find frozen Wooly Mammoths in this stuff all the time."

"Really? What do they do with the skins?"

"I have no freaking idea. The point is we should put on chains, so we don't slip into a ravine where they'll find *our* frozen asses in ten thousand years."

"I want a wooly mammoth coat. Damn, that would look good on stage. A little warm maybe, but I think I could rock the caveman look."

At the end of this road lies Steamboat Springs and a massive ski lodge where we will be opening for Cowboy Mouth. A warm fire and a nice Irish coffee would do me some good right now, but there is some question as to whether or not we are on the right track. In fact, there is some question as to whether we are actually in Colorado. The snow is so deep that the road signs are buried along with any landmarks highlighted on our maps. Regardless, we have no choice but to continue forward through this trench in the ice, like a needle in the groove of a giant white record.

I rub my hands together and hold them right up against the single heater vent on the passenger side. I wonder if Mia's aversion to the cold was somehow passed to me when we were married, like a dowry. Forget the Ferrari, when this album breaks, I'm buying a house with a fireplace. And space heaters. In Maui. Mia and the kid will never know a single shiver.

"Yo JT," I call to the back of the van, "you still have that wanker's card from Capitol Records?"

"Naw, I used it to light a joint back in Springdale."

"Are you fucking kidding me?"

"Of course I'm fucking kidding you."

"We should give him a call when we get to Steamboat Springs."

"Why? I thought we agreed we would give the independent band thing a try."

"We did."

"It's been, like, a month."

Ladd switches on the windshield wipers to deal with the dumping snowfall. The view through the window is like looking at a blank piece of paper. The black line that once defined the road is now light grey and disappearing fast.

"Dude, chains. Seriously," I say.

"Ok, I think ... What the hell is that?"

Up ahead in the distance, a thin brownish smudge appears on the horizon.

"Looks like smoke," I say.

JT and Eddie lean forward to get a better view through the windshield. "I'm not sure but I think it's coming toward us," says our new drummer. Indeed, the brown mass, vibrating slightly, is moving on a collision course. We all stare in fascination as tiny bits of detail begin to emerge until finally the mystery reveals itself.

"Cows," says JT. "Lots and lots of cows."

The herd of cattle, moving at a steady clip, fills the entire highway and most of the flatland on either side. Ladd eases on the brakes to no effect while the cows, oblivious to their inevitable bludgeoning by a two-ton steel box, continue to stampede directly at us.

Not only are the brakes useless, turning the wheel is an act of futility. With no control whatsoever we spin in a slow arc at 45 mph on the icy road until the side of the van and its accompanying trailer present itself to the oncoming mass of bovinity. I envision the van/trailer combination spinning through the herd, scattering beef tartare like a nunchuck in a slaughterhouse.

The distance between us closes in an instant. Moments before impact the surprise in the leading members' eyes is clearly visible, *Whoa, didn't see that coming.* I bow my head in empathy. Sorry guys, I know how it goes—more than one runaway van has smashed into my life, though mostly metaphorical in nature.

I brace myself against the dashboard, cringing in preparation for the inevitable thump and the potential flying cow to come sailing through the windshield. Once again, I regret the many stops at In-n-Out Burger, shuttering at the irony that my own demise might come at the hooves of an airborne cow.

Yet somehow, I don't die. In fact, no being dies, hoven or bipedal. The van spins and slides uncontrollably with the trailer jackknifed against the side but the anticipated bone crunching collision never occurs. The long dizzying spin executes its last slow revolution until we finally come to rest in the middle of the highway, quiet and anticlimactic.

I raise my head and open my eyes. A river of cattle flow around the van like Moses parting the beef sea, the dense snow and mist vomiting livestock from a seemingly endless source.

"Everyone ok?" asks JT.

Mumbles in the affirmative ripple through the van, but everyone's attention is on the bovine ocean surrounding us. I begin to wonder how we are going to get out of this when the herd finally thins and the last stragglers trot past the window.

"Well," says Ladd straightening the wheel, "that was interesting, but I think it is time..."

From seemingly nowhere a new creature stands before the van: a horse with a silhouetted rider sporting a wide brimmed cowboy hat and a Wyatt Earp-style ankle-length duster. Though the ghostly cowboy's features are completely hidden, 'tude radiates from his very existence. As we stare at him through the glass, I take note of the dark outline of a Winchester rifle tucked into a holster on the horse's shoulder.

"I don't think we should ask for directions," I say.

"Yeah," says JT, "this dude is definitely throwin' shade."

With the slightest flick of the cowboy's wrist the horse begins to move toward the passenger window. I sink a little into the seat as he draws near, but before he reaches the passenger side, inexplicably, he's gone.

"Where'd he go?" I ask turning my head to see the other side. Everyone checks through the van windows but no sign.

He's just gone.

I turn to Ladd with my best what-the-hell face, open the door and step out onto the freezing highway. I scan our surroundings, but visibility has dropped to about 50 feet.

Ladd appears next to me, head down and kicking snow around with his ancient Chucks. "Dude," he says as snowflakes gather in his long hair, "I'm no Texas Ranger or anything but something is weird here."

"What's that?"

"The snow. It's completely smooth," he says gazing around the van. "No tracks anywhere."

Holy shit.

"Maybe the snow covered the tracks," I offer.

"Maybe," says Ladd.

"Ok, we're not high, right? Didn't we just come within inches of prematurely tenderizing about five tons of beef?"

"Indeed we did. But who runs a herd of cattle down the middle of a highway into on-coming traffic and then gets mad when a van shows up?"

"I don't know. You don't see a Buddha around here do you?"

"A what?" asks Ladd.

"Nothing," I say, "Let's get out of here." I turn to climb back into the van before pausing at the door. "But first, chains. There may be actual, tangible obstacles ahead, or more cows of a less astral nature."

"I kinda talked to Capitol Records," says JT.

"What do you mean 'kinda?'" I ask.

"Imagine that you're calling someone who is on an airplane that is in the process of plummeting to the Earth from 30,000 feet."

"Difficulties at the label?"

"Apparently. That A&R guy we met in Austin was let go, and the receptionist I spoke with made it sound like the building was on fire. She was literally on the verge of tears."

"MP3's are bending over the entire industry. In some ways the karmic bludgeoning these ass wipes are taking is really gratifying, but on the other hand, how are you going to have rock star excess without excessive rock star money?"

"Keith Richard's transfusions aren't going to pay for themselves."

"Exactly."

JT came to the band with a song called "Bethany the Hot Chick that Works Behind the Counter at the Gap." Before he played a single note, I already knew it was the best song ever written, bar none, in the history of all mankind.

Thick with multiple layers, like poetic baclava, the title alone hints at an epic of Euclidian proportions. "Bethany," a moniker that can only be applied to a bitch-goddess of uncommon beauty, holds a position of authority at a retail establishment that is both loathed for its homogenization of style, yet ironically coveted as a gentrified alternative to the more proletariat offerings of a Target or Walmart.

One need only peel back the upper most layer to see that the protagonist has everything that young women want—beauty, power, poise, an employee discount—while dripping with an untouchable sexuality that sends tormented boys scrambling for hand lotion and a box of Kleenex. Ambition, lust, pathos, subtle notes of BDSM all wrapped up in a single sentence: "Bethany the Hot Chick that Works Behind the Counter at the Gap." Genius.

It turns out the tune was catchy too—a definite plus. While sitting at a Johnny Rockets sipping iced tea, my digestive system struggling with an ill-advised bacon cheeseburger, the song plays in an endless loop in my head. Serendipitously, the restaurant, is situated in the mall right across from a Gap store. Shoppers stream to and fro, hunting and gathering like their ancient ancestors only using dollars and shopping bags instead of flint knives and goat bladders, not to mention the convenience of an environment free of saber tooth tigers.

The need for a safe environment was a primary motivation for moving from our apartment in town to a tiny ranch-style house in suburbia. Mia and I were clueless in matters pertaining to raising a child, but our early exposure to TV suggested that fictional families like The Cosbys lived in suburban bliss, so that must be the best place to have a baby.

As newly-arrived suburban dwellers we replaced our frequent visits to cafes and bars with trips to the mall.

I look up at Mia, sitting across from me, beautifully round with our child.

"I wonder if there's a Bethany inside that store," I say.

"Like in JT's song? Of course there is." The corner of her mouth edges up as she leans in close to me. "Only she's a lesbian and no one knows. All the guys want her, but she's only interested in someone she can never have."

"The Prom Queen!" I announce.

Mia shakes her head. "Worse."

"Ms. Butchenson, the softball coach!"

"Worse."

"Not the Principal!?"

"No..." She leans in closer and whispers, "Her best friend's mom."

Scandalized, I raise my hand to my mouth. "Mrs. Robinson!"

We laugh over chili cheese fries, one of Mia's pregnancy cravings, and make up more stories about passersby. Mia proposes several theories on why an elderly gentleman is leaving a Victoria's Secret store with four giant shopping bags when the idea blooms in full.

"Malltopia," I interrupt.

"What's that?" she asks.

"That is the name of our next record. I think we should do a concept album based on a day at the mall—a modern epic with an Orange Julius Caesar."

"I love it," says Mia. "There's a nasty Gyro place down at the far end. If that isn't a Greek Tragedy, I don't know what is."

With *Malltopia* we surrender to the digital revolution. Instead of booking a recording studio we buy one that is delivered to my house in a cardboard box. We set it up in my garage, ignoring the thick stacks of manuals which comprise the bulk of the package contents. When the last cable is fitted to its last color-coded input, we ceremoniously flip a small switch on the back the unit.

The screen flares to life revealing a virtual world of limitless possibilities. We poke at the keyboard like children playing chopsticks on a piano, exposing infinite pathways to manipulate sound.

"Wow, check this out, you can quantize the drum track."

"Really? What does that mean?"

"I have no idea."

"What do you suppose an 'L2 Utramaximizer' does?"

"I'm not sure, but we should definitely ultra-maximize everything on the album."

And so it began.

Ninety percent of our recording knowledge was now obsolete, and we would have to start over from the beginning. Our aversion to reading instructions didn't help much either. With great power comes great opportunity to suck, and we spent a full month just trying to get a vocal to not sound like it was coming through my dog's ass.

We eventually gave up on the drums. We just emailed the tracks to Eddie in New Orleans and he recorded his parts ol' skool in a proper, upstanding Baptist studio. The ecclesiastic performances lent a welcome air of analog salvation to the project.

Aside from digital ineptitude, recording in one's garage presents other unforeseen challenges. My neighbor's lawn sprinklers are audible on several tracks along with barking dogs, loud televisions, and worst of all, passing boom-trucks with earthquake inducing sub-woofers.

At one point, while laying down a vocal for "Food Court Rockstar," a grating, murderous scream emanates from across the street. I glance at JT who's engineering the session while I record my part. Though no words pass between us we both understand the dilemma: Do we have some inherent responsibility to investigate evidence of intense human suffering or can we just blow it off and keep on working?

With a long sigh of resignation, I remove my headphones and step out the door. In my driveway I am met by my middle-aged neighbor, Lois, who is brandishing a .357 Magnum in one hand and half of a dead cat in the other. Holding the half-cat by the tail she levels the hand cannon at my chest and screams, "I'M GOING TO KILL THAT BITCH!"

Damn. I knew we shoulda' kept working.

"Hey Lois," I say in my calmest Mr. Roger's Neighborhood voice, "why don't you put down the gun and we'll get this all figured out. Come on inside and let's have some coffee." Mia is allergic to cats and that probably applies to half-cats as well, but I'm more allergic to bullets so I'm sure Mia will understand.

"FUCK YOU" she screams. "FUCK ALL OF YOU!" She waves the gun around at the neighborhood.

People who had gathered in their doorways to watch the show retreat into their houses, though many eyes appear on the lower edges of windowsills.

"You wanna know what that bitch did?" Lois asks stepping right up to me. "She let that ferocious pit bull out, a menace to the whole goddamn neighborhood, and look what it did!" She holds the half-cat up to my face. "You all knew that dog was dangerous BUT NOBODY DID ANYTHING ABOUT IT!" She pokes me in the ribs with her gun barrel to accentuate her point.

"Look, Lois..."

"DON'T EVEN TALK TO ME!" she screams, raising the gun up to my face. Looking down the barrel I meet her bloodshot eye, wide with pain and loathing.

"Oh Lois," says a sympathetic voice behind me, "your poor cat ... She was so beautiful. You know, we have cats..."

Oh no. No! No! No!

Up until this moment, though a bit unsettled, I felt I had things under control. But Mia's appearance on the scene brings an immediate sense of terror and panic the likes of which I had never before experienced. This *cannot* be happening. I brought my wife and our unborn child here to be safe, to live in vanilla tranquility among mowed lawns and Bermuda shorts. But now my whole life, my entire reason for living, rests in the trembling hand of an insane cat lady brandishing a weapon that put the "dirty" in Dirty Harry.

My knees almost buckle as I watch the long chrome barrel swivel to Mia.

I could go all Jackie Chan at this point, grabbing the gun and decking the Old Bat with an elbow to the larynx, but I know what will happen. The gun will go off, killing us both, while the bullet ricochets into the gas tank of the Ford Taurus across the street resulting in a fireball that burns the entire neighborhood to the ground, killing everyone except the kids playing in the park who become orphaned homeless street urchins living in drainpipes for the rest of their short, insufferable lives.

No. Heroics are not my forte.

Slowly, with my palms spread wide, I step into the gap between the gun and my wife.

"Mia, please go back into the house." I try to sound authoritarian, but it comes out pleading.

She ignores me, continuing her narrative. "You know our cats, Monterey Jack and Mild Cheddar, I've seen you give them treats. I don't know what I would do if anything happened to them."

We don't have cats and I have no idea what she's going on about.

"Oh Mia," says Lois, tears streaming down her face, "look, look what happened to my baby!" She holds the half-cat out for Mia to inspect.

"Oh Lois, honey, I am so, so sorry."

Lois breaks down completely and to my horror Mia moves in with open arms. As she wraps Lois in one arm, she gently removes the gun from our neighbor's flaccid hand and passes it to me behind her back. Holding the firearm with two fingers I look around for a place to set it before finally slipping it into the mailbox and closing the door.

In the distance I hear the sound of sirens steadily increasing in volume—the cavalry arriving too late. As the squad cars come screeching into the neighborhood Mia continues to embrace Lois. Pleasant Hill's finest scramble out with hands on their sidearms, running up our driveway while I hold my palms in the air and attempt to calm the situation.

"It's cool guys, everything is cool."

After a lot of scribbling on notepads and neighbors coming over to relive the tale from their vantage points, the cops finally leave with the gun but not with Lois. No one wants to press any charges nor deal with her densely packed cat hotel.

As we wander back into the house, shock and fear transition into anger. How could Mia, in her condition, be so foolish as to walk into such an obviously dangerous situation? I turn to vent my ire when she hauls off and slugs me in the arm.

"What the hell were you thinking!" she shouts, "Who goes outside to have a neighborly chat with a crazy lady waving around a dead cat and a gun?"

I rub my shoulder, surprised and confused. "What the hell was *I* thinking? What the hell were *you* thinking!"

Tears form in the corners of her eyes before she flies into me, wrapping her arms around my waist so tightly I can barely breath. "Oh my god when I looked out the window and saw that gun pointed at you, I just ran out there to clock that bitch."

"That could have ended poorly," I say, stroking her hair.

"The half-cat thing threw me off. I figured a lighter approach would be more effective."

"There you are," says JT wandering in through the garage door. "I finally got a guitar take I think is worth ... What's up, you guys ok?"

"You didn't see that?" I say with Mia's face buried in my shoulder.

"See what? I was wearing headphones ... I got a good take."

Mia turns to JT. "Your brother thinks he's Jean-Claude Van Damme" she says, whipping away her tears.

"More like Chuck Norris," I say.

Despite a long, grueling trek over the learning curve, *Malltopia* emerges from the garage in all its glossy digital glory. The sessions yield neither cassette nor CD. It's an intangible computer file whose very existence is circumspect—ones and zeros strung together in such a fashion that, if exposed to the right software on the right device, will emit kickass songs. In the words of William Shakespeare, "What devil art thou?"

We send it out to the Usual Suspects looking for feedback and opportunities. Our long-time friend, Bob Chiaparti, at Concrete Marketing in New York calls us with an idea. He loves the album's concept and introduces us to a contact from an industry completely foreign to us: a Broadway producer.

Within days of the album's release, JT and I are hunkered down at a Starbucks hashing out story lines despite having never been to Broadway itself. As kids we had both seen the movie version of *Paint Your Wagon*, so we figured we were fully qualified.

We had a blast unraveling the mysteries of Bethany, the Hot Chick that Worked Behind the Counter at the Gap, but alas, like so many music business opportunities, it died a quick, vapid death. The Producer was offered millions of dollars in funding for another project, and dollars, millions or otherwise, were something The Uninvited could not compete with. I tucked our Tony award away in the Vault of Impossibility and closed the door with a sigh.

Atomic Love Bomb

"All the tears that filled up tissues
Are blow away by other issues
Swept beneath the carpets of my mind"
- The Ghost of Sigmund Freud, The Uninvited

"I feel something," says Mia.

Thank God, it's about time.

We had been languishing on this suburban sofa for two weeks waiting for our nuclear family to expand. I postponed the tour so I could be here for the baby's arrival, but he's running late. I assumed he would be eager to get here—his newly painted bedroom is stuffed to the ceiling with grandparent-supplied baby technology and toys specifically designed to turn ordinary infants into Gold Medal Olympian Neurosurgeons.

Mia puts her hand on her belly while I check my watch to time the contractions. Over the last few weeks we have taken enough baby delivery classes that I now have a PhD in Tell Her To Breath. Sure enough, the contractions are coming at the magic interval—hospital time.

In a rush of excitement, I grab the pre-packed overnight bag complete with all necessary items—thank you, Baby Delivery Class—and gently, calmly escort my wife to our pre-fueled, recently serviced automobile resplendent with a spanking new bomb-proof infant seat.

I drive swiftly, yet safely, along the pre-planned route to the hospital, telling Mia to breath between contractions. I got this.

Grimacing in pain, my wife informs me that breathing is an autonomic function of the nervous system. Reminders are not only unnecessary, but actually quite annoying in sufficient numbers.

At the hospital we are met with little fanfare. I'm not sure what I was expecting, maybe a crack medical team in scrubs gathered around a waiting gurney, but all we get is a bored receptionist and a clipboard:

"Fill this out and someone will be with you shortly."

An eternity later a nurse steps up to Mia with another clipboard, "How are you feeling?"

"Great," says Mia.

"When was the last contraction?"

Mia glances around for a moment before her eyes settle on me. "Hmm, I don't remember the last one. I think they stopped."

We drive home along the pre-planned route.

Back on the sofa I'm hoping David Letterman might say something to coax our son into born-ness, but it is not to be.

Later, we slump into bed tired and disappointed with words of encouragement to the little guy. My last offer is $100 before sleep overtakes us.

"It's time. We really need to go," says Mia.

I bolt upright in bed, eyes wide with adrenaline, a foreign edge in Mia's voice focusing my attention. I carefully bundle her up, wrap a supporting arm around her waist, and half-carry her to the car. She is quiet on the drive. I can't see her face, only occasional glimpses as we pass under streetlights. Eyes closed; she grips my hand with an unfamiliar intensity.

We arrive at the hospital squinting in sanitary florescent light. The waiting room is empty. It's late, or early, I'm not sure which. An elderly midwife emerges from an unseen door bearing all the usual questions. Mia answers with distracted listlessness; the midwife nods while pressing the end of a stethoscope to various parts of my wife's stomach.

"Ok," she says removing the device from her ears, "let's go have a baby."

Her smile strikes me as an act of professionalism.

We are escorted to a room crowded with medical equipment. They lay Mia on the bed and tape sensors to her body. Machines light up with graphs and numbers, people in gowns shuffle about purposefully, and I try to stay out of the way.

Mia grimaces, lifting her head from the pillow. I navigate a path to her bedside and take her hand, trying to deal with a sense of uselessness. Classes, books, and advice evaporate, they are meaningless in the face of reality. I pull her hand to my chest and place my forehead against hers, willing the pain to stop.

Events progress quickly and within the hour contractions are coming in rapid succession. Nurses dressed in teddy bear print offer words of encouragement at the foot of the bed, but my gaze never leaves her face.

"Almost there, Baby, one more push..."

"We need the doctor," someone says, "quickly."

A list of other required items is rattled off, but I'm too tired and confused to parse the meaning. Activity increases in the room, equipment, and personnel crowd the small space, but all talking stops as the doctor, a detectable edge in his voice, issues orders and instructions.

Our son's arrival is beautiful, yet strangely quiet. I have no experience with birth, but I know it is supposed to be noisy. The nurse briefly holds up our son, but before I can get a good look at his face it is covered with a tiny respirator. It looks like a toy.

"Is everything ok?"

Either no one hears me, or no one wants to answer. The quiet, still newborn is hastily wrapped in a blanket, placed on a steel tray, and rolled from the room.

"Where is he?" whispers Mia.

"I think they're checking on him..." My attempt to sound reassuring rings false in my own ears.

She looks up at me, but I feel as though she doesn't see me. I move a wet strand of hair from her face, surprised by the coolness of her skin. "You feel cold, would you like another blanket?"

She continues to stare at me, unseeing, until her eyes roll up in her head and her hand drops from my chest.

A diminishing opacity of the dark moments of our lives is one of the few merciful aspects of the passage of time. Looking back, I remember little of what happened next—a hand on my arm pulling me from the room, a faint sound of buzzers. I have a picture of her, a faded mental snapshot. Tubes, wires, and stained bedding do nothing to distract from her beauty.

I sit in an orange plastic chair across from a vending machine. White walls and a white Formica floor reflect cold florescent light. The faint smell of alcohol and burnt coffee lingers. I am alone save for an elderly lady sitting five chairs down pressing two Kleenexes to both of her eyes.

Inside the vending machine, behind the glass, a granola bar triggers a memory of standing outside a pool hall in Venice Beach. I walk over to the machine and place my forehead against the glass, recalling a four-year-old act of kindness. Reaching into my pocket I pull out a handful of change and start feeding coins into the slot indiscriminately until I have no more left to give. I select the granola bar, watch it fall to the bottom, and remove it from the box.

Stepping over to the room's only other occupant, I hold out the bar.

"Excuse me, ma'am, can I offer you this?"

The elderly lady removes a tissue just long enough to glance at the package and shakes her head. "No thank you."

"Are you sure, ma'am? I've seen these do some good."

She removes both tissues, looks up and studies my face with red, swollen eyes. "That's very nice of you young man," she says accepting the offering, "It's not for me, but I know a little girl who could use it." She tucks it away in her purse as I drift back to my chair to sit down.

My mind is blank. I don't want to think. I don't want to contemplate. I don't want anything to do with this moment at all.

The sound of footsteps in the hall brings a reprieve from empty thoughts. I look up to see my brother standing in the doorway with a mylar balloon and a bouquet of flowers. Our eyes meet and his smile vanishes. The flowers drop to his side.

"Jesus Bro, what's going on?"

I get up to explain but I can't coax any words from mouth. I glance around, as though I might find some words lying around the room, when he places a hand on my shoulder. I am the older brother, so I struggle to maintain a facade of strength, but it's gone.

Everything is gone.

"Mr. Taylor?"

I turn to see a nurse with a teddy bear surgical mask pulled down around her neck.

"Yes."

"I have an update for you. Your wife lost a lot of blood, but we have it under control. She's a little weak but she's going to be fine."

My knees fail and I slump back into the chair. But before I surrender to relief, I lift my head. "And my son?"

It's the first time I ever used those words. They feel weighty and wonderous.

"He has meconium aspiration, meaning he inhaled a fluid passed from the intestine while in the uterus or during labor. He's on a respirator in the Neonatal Intensive Care Unit now. We're doing everything we can."

"Will he be ok?"

She pauses, considering her words. "It's a severe case. We'll know in the next 24 hours."

. . .

I carefully maneuver Mia down the hall in a wheelchair, working our way around medical personnel and equipment until we reach the NICU. The attendant shows us to a clear plastic tray where our child, Dax, lays wrapped in a blanket on a thin pad, a large tube snaking into his throat. Smaller tubes and wires disappear into his wrapping. We're allowed to touch him, but we can't hold him. With visible effort Mia rises from her wheelchair, places a hand on his chest, and closes her eyes.

"Is he in pain?" she asks the attendant.

"No, we have him on a morphine drip to keep him from choking on the respirator," answers the nurse.

Tears run freely down my wife's cheeks landing in small droplets on the baby's blanket. She takes my hand, leans into me, and settles back into the chair, her head falling on a pillow I placed against the headrest.

"Ok, let's get you back to bed," I say, positioning myself behind her wheelchair.

"No," she says shaking her head. "I am not going anywhere. The doctors say we'll know in 24-hours. There is no way on Earth that I am leaving his side until I know he's not going to ... until I know he's safe." Even with half her blood gone and her body ravaged by childbirth, the tone of her voice makes it clear she would win this fight.

Surrendering, I raise my hands from her chair and pull up a stool. Taking her hand, I raise it to my lips, and settle in to wait it out.

The windowless ICU offers no natural light; I am clueless as to whether it's day or night. The staff is sympathetic to Mia's insistence on not returning to her room, so a nurse comes in occasionally to take her blood pressure and give us food. The latest meal was chicken and vegetables, microwaved into a paste, so I'm guessing it's evening.

As Mia dozes in her chair, I stand next to our baby's acrylic container and place my hand on top of his tiny head. "Jeez little man," I whisper, "this has got to be the sorriest excuse for a bassinet I have ever seen." I stare at his face, mesmerized. "You did luck out in one way though; you got your mom's good looks."

The now familiar feeling of uselessness rises again. I have been nothing more than a witness to the events as they unfold, unable to help or protect or prevent.

I lean in close to my 6-hour-old son. "I suppose I should introduce myself: I am your Dad." I pick up his little hand with two fingers and move it up and down. "That's the first time I have ever used that phrase and I really want to be able to use it again. I am so sorry for the bumpy start with this whole life thing—it gets better—I'll make sure it gets better. But this part right now, you just have to power through it. I know you're cold and confused and probably terrified, but I'm right here, Little Man, right here next to you.

"I have absolutely no experience with this dad thing, but I have a lot of experience from your side of the relationship, and the way it works is you have to do what Dad says. It sucks sometimes but that's the way it is. So, I am telling you, right now as your Dad, you have to stay with us, okay? You hang on Little Man and you hang on *tight*. We have some great times ahead of us, but you have to push through this. I am your Dad, and you have to do what I say."

When I was 7-years-old, my father asked me to sweep the porch one sunny Saturday morning. The injustice was dumbfounding. Though the porch was only 50 square feet at most, to my 7-year-old perspective the surface was an infinite plateau of dirt that stretched to the farthest most reaches of the horizon, like being asked to sweep Wyoming.

Besides, I had other plans.

Unbeknownst to my parents I was already deep into my project of dismantling the garage in order to construct a pirate ship. We lived not too far from Mission Bay in San Diego, and the plan was to launch my ship in the calm waters of the bay, sail up the coast a short distance to the wealthy community of La Jolla Shores, then lob a few cannon balls into the mansions lining the beach with the goal of persuading the local gentry to part with whatever treasure they may have laying about.

Thus, not only did I have to finish the ship, but there were all kinds of logistical details still needing to be ironed out. Do my brothers and I have enough wagons to get my ship to the water? Where does one hire a crew of cutthroats? Do I have enough gun powder in my firecracker collection to launch the requisite cannonade?

No, sweeping the porch would not fit into this weekend's agenda.

"Sorry Dad, I'm really busy."

At the time, Dad was attending college while working full-time and trying to raise three kids. I once heard him complain to my grandfather that he would be 30-years-old before he graduated. My grandfather told him he was going to be 30 regardless. He could be 30 and have a college diploma, or he could just be 30.

Dad knew a thing or two about being busy and didn't need any 'tude from a deluded 7-year-old pirate.

Though he never laid a hand on us, he had a look. If Darth Vader could express incredulity, that would be the gaze that the fell upon my quaking, 7-year-old head.

I sheepishly retreated to the closet, procured the broom, and headed out to the patio. There, under the weight of immeasurable oppression, I slowly pushed around a small clump of dirt, contemplating my eventual demise on this endless, plywood wasteland. After an hour of toil in abject misery, my father walked out of the house on his way to work.

"Jesus Son, are you still here? Give me that."

He grabbed the broom out my hand and leaned into the task. "First you get the corners and move the dirt to the center..." The broom was a blur, the bristles bent at a 45-degree angle. "Run along all the edges, until the dirt is all in the center..." He scooped up the dustpan in one quick motion. "Now you have the dirt in a manageable pile. We sweep it into the pan, now into the trash, and that's it, you're done."

He handed the broom back to me as I gazed about, flabbergasted. The whole job took less than 20 seconds. "Listen," he said, "if you got a job to do you can't stand around moping about how unfair life is. Just get it done and get on with your life." He pulled me in and kissed me on top of my head. "Now go have fun."

Mia and I awake to the sound of the doctor's voice: "Mr. and Mrs. Taylor?"

My neck is cramped from leaning against the wall while dozing on the stool.

"We have an update about your son. He's responding remarkably well to treatment and I am very happy with his progress. We'll need to keep him here for another week or so, but I am confident he'll be able to go home soon."

When I bought my first car, the salesman guided me through every feature on the vehicle before handing me a thick manual, a maintenance schedule, and finally the keys. But when the hospital gives you a human being, you just sign a piece of paper and leave.

Mia and I bring Dax home for the first time, introduce him to Ashlei, and set him on a pillow in the middle of the floor.

I turn to Mia and say, "I have absolutely no idea what to do."

"Oh honey," she says laughing, "it's just a baby. It's easy."

She was wrong.

A sharp elbow catches me in the ribs. "Your turn," says a far-off voice.

My turn? Impossible. Either I'm stuck in some kind of freakish time loop or Mia is gaming me. My left ear is not everything it used to be thanks to 10 years of Bruce's crash symbol. The one upside to hearing loss is it allows you to sleep through a lot of racket, but right now Dax's wailing makes Bruce's symbol sound like a wind chime.

With Herculean Effort I manage to crawl out of bed and drag my feet to our son's crib. I subconsciously tuck him under my arm like a football, the only way he wants to be carried, and move the screaming package to the living room. I had a vague understanding that newborns didn't sleep through the night, but Dax's problem was compounded by the fact that he was suffering from morphine withdraws after coming off the respirator. At only two weeks old our son is a recovering junkie.

With one practiced hand I nuke his bottle of breast milk while cradling him like a quarterback in the other. I hold the bottle in his mouth and begin the Dax Dance, a unique series of movements required to make him fall asleep. Sitting down, rocking chair or otherwise, is not acceptable and he will *let you know it*. If all else fails, I will be forced to launch into 20 to 30 verses of "Build Me Up Buttercup," but that's a last resort as it has to be sung at a volume that will wake the neighbors.

I feel the slightest nudge against my leg and look down to find Ashlei, subtly reminding me that yes, she still exists. Holding

Dax's bottle up with my chin I dig around in the cupboard with my free hand until I find her milk-bones.

"Sorry Old Girl," I say tossing her the treat, "First me and now Dax. A lot of usurpers in this house, hogging up all the attention."

And so our ritual continues, night after night, day after day, as our baby's morphine-addled sleep pattern has him napping for 20 minutes an hour, 24 hours a day.

Within a few weeks Mia has to return to work, shuffling out the door and into the evening like a character from *Dawn of the Dead*. At night I try to take as many bottle calls as possible so she can get enough rest to maintain the illusion of coherency at work. We occasionally see each other in the hall during baby handoff, but our interaction is everything one might expect from zombie roommates.

When JT calls with news of our upcoming tour, panic and relief battle for dominance. The thought of four hours of uninterrupted sleep in a broken, cushionless car seat is as welcomed as a week-long stay at the Hotel La Perouse on the French Riviera. The future arrival of the van heralds a return to music, adventure, and glorious re-admittance into the human race.

But there is a problem: it's two feet long and wants to be held like a football 24-hours a day. Even with help from the grandparents, relatives, and friends, I have no idea how Mia will survive while I'm gone. "It takes a village…" is how the saying goes, but in our case, it requires the Greater San Francisco Metropolitan Area.

The night before the van arrives, Dax gets up for the third or fourth time around 4 a.m. I have not slept at all, so it is not difficult to roll out of bed and scoop him up. I prepare his bottle, look at his perfect face and begin our slow waltz.

"I am so torn up I can't count the pieces," I whisper to my son. "Dads are supposed to be these invincible pillars but I'm afraid I'm fucking it up right out of the gate. Your mom's dad, your grandpa, used to say, 'There is nothing more important than family.' So how can I leave you and Mom when you need me? But your JT, your uncle, he's family too, and without me, a lot of dreams and work go right into the toilet—a modern convenience I hope you learn to use soon."

An expression flickers across his face. Maybe it's just gas, but I'm overcome with a feeling that he hears me.

"I made a mistake, Son. I promised your mom so much— massive pie-in-the-sky dreams. I so desperately wanted her to … Well, I wanted her. This life that takes me away from you guys is the only way I stand a chance of even coming close to fulfilling those promises. Without it, that pie-in-the-sky might as well be pie on Alpha Centauri. And what else would I do? Join the pocket-protector crowd down in Silicon Valley? Sit in front of a keyboard for the rest of my life? Your mom didn't marry that guy. If I stop doing this then the whole façade falls to the ground and I'm just … I don't know what I am."

The van pulls up, the horn honks, the beckoning door slides open. I kiss Little Man on the head, scratch Ashlei under her greying chin, and plant a long goodbye on Mia's lips—a hint of resignation with notes of distraction. She smiles as I pull away, sensing my reticence.

"We're going to be fine," she says. "Stop worrying. Everything is setup and I have all the help I need. We've been over this a thousand times, now go do your thing and stop worrying about us." She puts her hand on my chest and applies the slightest pressure.

Stepping into the van I'm surprised to find JT alone behind the wheel. Usually T-Money is driving and I'm the last stop for pickup.

"Hey Bro," I say, "where's Tony?" JT looks over my shoulder and waves at Mia holding Dax in the doorway. She waves back before disappearing into the house.

"What are we doing?" says JT.

"I thought we were going to Vegas..."

JT continues to stare at my front door for several seconds.

"You don't want to be here," he says. I can't tell if the statement is advice or mind reading. "Bro," he says turning to me, "you already won. You brought home the Grand Prize and set it up right here. What are you looking for out there?" He holds his open palm out to the windshield. "Success? Admiration? Acceptance? The fleeting attention of the masses? Why? You already have the real thing."

I fidget about in my seat trying to find a comfortable position before giving up and letting my head fall back on the headrest. "I'm afraid of losing the 'real thing.'"

"No way," sighs JT. "I know what love looks like, trust me, I learned the hard way, and it looks like *this*." He nods toward my front door. "You're not going to lose anything by being in her bed in the morning when she wakes up. She wants *you* and could care less about some persona packaged for mass consumption."

"Besides," he says staring out the windshield, "it doesn't matter what she wants, or what you want or what I want. Our wants are trumped by the needs of the bigger 'We.' This fluffy, WASPY culture we live in, we have no 'coming of age' ritual, no dividing line between boy and man. But one thing is for certain, you stop being a kid as soon as you make one. It's taken me a couple years to realize that." He turns to face me. "You and I, Bro, it's time to grow up."

The last note of the last song of the last show of the last tour of the last great one-hit-wonder bands of the twentieth century rings through the Black Diamond Brewery until it's engulfed in an outpouring of emotion from an invite-only audience of fans, friends, and family.

"Thank you everyone, thank you so much."

The venue closes but no one goes home. The owners, long-time friends of the band, open the bar to those who are not yet ready to say goodbye, and the stories and laughter carry on fueled by alcohol.

Bill, who joined us on-stage for the last show, reaches behind the bar and pulls out a bottle of Jack Daniels along with two shot glasses. "Fuck you for introducing me to this stuff," he says pouring to the top of the glasses.

I raise my drink in a salute and gulp down the burning liquid. "Damn, I'm still sorry about that night, Bill."

"That's okay," he says with a grin. "Those were some of the best times of my life, and quite honestly, I wouldn't change a single moment." He smiles knowingly. "But the show is not really over my friend, not over by a long shot."

I stare at him blankly, having no idea what he's talking about.

"Also, fuck you, you're paying for all my drinks tonight."

As the sun comes up over Highway 680, I steer for the exit that leads home, having dropped off the rest of the band at their respective apartments. As I make the last turn, I notice I forgot someone, or something.

There, still laying on his side upon the dashboard, is The Gnome.

"Jesus, I forgot all about you, you little bastard."

I take a quick detour and drive the van back to the old neighborhood where I picked up the statuette years before. The house looks exactly the same, complete with the little bench, empty, and the inexplicable primordial dragonfly still keeping vigil over the manicured lawn.

I slowly maneuver the van up to the front of the house, careful not to awaken anyone inside. I really don't want to have to explain, at 5 a.m., that I am the freak who stole their lawn gnome and drove him around the country photographing him with bottles of gin and truck stop hookers and ... Oh, by the way, how did he get to be such a dick?

I grab The Gnome by his face and quietly trek across the lawn to the little bench. Gently, almost ceremoniously, I set him down on the weathered wood, step back, and study the scene. Sprinklers, birds, and the sounds of waking suburbia stir in the distance, but The Gnome has nothing to say. It turns out he's just plaster and paint.

Epillogue

The score was 6 to 7.

An eight-year-old boy, his long blonde hair hanging in his eyes, could not believe the ball was hurling his way. He held up his hands, more in a defensive gesture than a catching position, but somehow the orange rubber orb tucked right in between his palms. No one ever threw him the ball, and if they did, it usually just bounced off some part of his body.

But not this time.

For the tiniest moment he gazed upon the ball in his hands with both awe and fear. He glanced over his shoulder at the impossibly far away basket while his tongue probed a swollen, salty cut he received earlier in the game courtesy of an elbow on the opposing team. He was well aware of the score and the fact that they were behind. Only six short seconds remained in the game, but the basket was *miles* away.

Frantically, he searched the court for his teammates, desperate to get rid of this time bomb ticking away in his hands. Unbelievably, no familiar jersey caught his eye. No help anywhere, just the bright green shirts of the opposing team forming an impenetrable wall. He was stuck. He would lose the ball. He thought about disappointing everyone—again. He could see each of their disgusted faces, feel the weak touch of the coach's lame high five.

"Nice try. Good effort."

A familiar choked-up feeling rose in his throat and his eyes began to fill.

But the blond haired boy, smallest on the team, shook the dark thoughts from his head. "To hell with it," he said to himself.

He wasn't supposed to use that word, but he didn't care. Taking a breath and turning on his heel he found a gap and ran for the basket at the far side of the court, his right hand barely able to control the high bounces he pumped with every stride. The boy knew his limitations—the only thing he could really dribble was a chocolate shake down the front of his shirt—but maybe he could just get a little closer.

In ten strides he was right under the net. He stopped, marveling in the fact that he still held the ball and looked to his right where his teammates should be standing, arms stretched in the universal "Over here!" stance, but all he saw was the palm of a hand forming a wide-spread five just two inches from his nose—stuck again.

The chocking fear rose in his throat as he wrapped his body around the ball like a prawn, but somehow the sound of his frenetic teammates finally registered:

"Shoot! Shoot! Shoot!"

He looked up toward the backboard, but a canopy of arms and hands blocked the basket from view. He shifted his weight to his right, pivoted on the ball of his foot, squeezed under the arm of the closest defender, and blindly tossed the ball up in the air.

The buzzer blasted in shrill finality.

The smallest boy on the team, enraptured by the arc of the ball, watched as it hit the rim, bounced up, hit the backboard, and fell right through the net.

Pandemonium.

He couldn't even hear his own scream of triumph as his fists shot into the air. Instantly his teammates were all over him, slapping his back, lifting him off the ground, screaming in his ear. Through the gaps in the crowd he scanned the stands, looking for someone.

Three rows up, there he was, Dad, going absolutely batshit.

"Did you see that!" the boy yelled, knowing full well his father could not possibly hear him over the chaos in the gym. "Did you see it!?"

But it was obvious. Dad was freaking out, slapping the other dads on the back and pointing at the scoreboard. He definitely saw it.

He saw everything.

One Last Story

*"We can drink up this wine
We can talk about things
Like the distance between
Our lives and our dreams"*
-In the Company of Losers, The Uninvited

In the waning days of The Uninvited, I noticed a face that would appear at random shows all over the country. He would be in Athens, GA one night and Releigh, NC the next, then show up a few days later in Austin, TX. It seemed odd to me that someone would follow the band like that considering the time and expense. Honestly, there were nights even I didn't want to show up for a gig. Yet even on those nights, there he was in the back, smiling and bobbing his head over a beer.

One night in New York I finally met him. His name was Danny and it turned out that he was one of Our Man Tony's best friends. I bought him a drink in exchange for the story of why and how he made it to so many shows all over the county, and was amazed at the beautiful, yet tragic circumstances that placed him on this bar stool next to me.

Danny was born with his heart turned backwards. There's a medical term for it that I have since forgotten, but the bottom line for Danny, according to the doctors at the time, was that he wouldn't live past 18.

So, at 16, knowing he didn't have much time, Danny married his high school sweetheart. Shortly after that, he miraculously got a job as a software developer for IBM where he quickly rose through ranks. "Genius" is a word people apply much too casually, but in this case it is the only word that fits. Within three minutes I knew I was in the presence of a unique individual with a deep and profound intellect, and wisdom far beyond his years.

On Danny's 18th birthday... he didn't die.

He woke up that morning slightly surprised, but knew it was a gift.

Every day he would wake up after that birthday was a miracle, a treasure to be exploited to its fullest.

During his tenure at IBM, he saw that the company was throwing out a piece of old software that was no longer profitable. Sensing an opportunity, he bought the application for next to nothing. And within a few short years he took that worthless piece of software and built a multi-million-dollar company in Austin, Texas that employed hundreds of people.

But Danny didn't bury himself in work. He was literally on borrowed time, so if he wanted to have lunch in Paris with his wife, he just went and did it. If his favorite band wasn't in town, he would just go to wherever the band was.

A few months later, when The Uninvited announced our farewell tour, Danny called me.

"Hey, what are you going to do now?" he asked.

"Honestly, I have no idea," I answered.

"Well in that case, you should come work for me," he said. "Tell me what you're interested in. You can do whatever you want."

I was speechless. Having no idea how to respond to such an unexpected and generous offer, all I could say was, "Really? Why me?"

"You and your brother's music have done so much for me, I want to do something for you in return."

Grateful and humbled, I told him I was always interested in web development, but I had no experience whatsoever and wouldn't even know where to start.

"Great," he said. "You are now officially in charge of our website. I'll book you a flight to Austin and you can come meet the team. By the way, I just hired your brother in our marketing department. Welcome aboard!"

Terrified and in over my head, I flew to Austin. Danny picked me up at the airport and drove us straight to a local bookstore without stopping. Once there he started pulling web development books off the shelf and piling them in my arms. "It's not rocket science," he said. "Just read these and you'll be fine."

I was not fine.

I was stressed out of my mind. People go to college to learn this stuff, and I had no business being at these developer meetings. I was supposed to be building a new website for a hugely successful software company with zero knowledge and a borrowed laptop.

But stress, coffee, and 16-hour work days, combined with the need to feed my new family, eventually resulted in a passable website. And when that site finally went live, I was able to add a second line to my resume:

1. Pretty good at tuning a guitar.
2. Web Developer.

A few years later, Danny passed away during an experimental surgery to try to fix his condition. His death left a big hole in many lives, but anyone who knew him was also blessed with an invaluable gift: the knowledge that every day matters.

I still miss him. To this very day, every time I finish a new website, I pour myself the now rare gin & tonic and raise my glass to the man who had enough love and faith to take a chance on a clueless guitarist with a broken dream.

When The Uninvited broke up, I took Mia back to her home in Maui, Hawaii where we raised our two children 3000 feet up the side of a dormant volcano called Haleakala. The kids became musicians themselves. Their young bands would bang away on Beatles and AC/DC songs in our garage, filling our tropical nights with music and complaining neighbors. Mia used to joke, "This is what happens when you have sex with a musician. More musicians."

The bulk of this book was written on note pads sitting by The Cove at Baldwin, or Baby Beach in Makena, or Grammas Beach on the West Side. Originally, I framed the story as "an epic face plant at 100 miles-per-hour leaving a 30-yard skid mark ending two inches short of the finish line."

A glorious failure.

But as I relived the 20-year-old events sitting in the shade of kiawe trees and listening to the surf, I quickly realized that everything I am, everything I have, everything I became was a direct result of my friends and I reaching out for something one-inch on the other side of impossible.

The Uninvited was not my greatest failure.

It was my greatest achievement.

And while the stupid pen I used to sign my first record deal kept dying, a long-dormant yearning returned.

Mia and I missed friends and family on the mainland, and the kids wanted to attend college in California. And by "attend college," I mean take a few classes while pursuing what is apparently a genetic desire for a music career.

So, following a 10-year-adventure in the most remote island chain in the world, we packed up and moved back to the Bay Area. Within a week of our arrival, knowing that every day matters, I started making calls. And much like Jake and Elwood in *The Blues Brothers,* I got right to the point:

"Hey, we're putting the band back together..."

Bill Cory   John Taylor   Steve Taylor   Bruce Logan

The Uninvited

Promotional 8x10 for Atlantic Records. Bill, JT, Steve and Bruce.

Steve and Bill screaming for no apparent reason at the world-famous
Troubadour in Hollywood.

Bill Cory and his overgrown mohawk.

Bruce Logan, the only professional musician in the band.

Eddie Ecker bringing some New Orleans cool to the band after Bruce
Logan left.

JT bringing the thunder

JT and bassist Ladd Story at the KROCK festival. Ladd's second
show with the band.

The Uninvited playing at the 1999 MTV Video Awards block party

JT and Steve at the Santa Monica pier on the night Steve asked out
Mia for the first time.

Steve and JT at the House of Blues in Las Vegas

JT and Steve at the KROCK festival in New York

Steve and Mia backstage at the House of Blues in Hollywood, shortly after Steve mangled his conversation with Tori Amos.

Clay Goldstein (harmonica), Bill Cory, Steve Taylor, JT with a mutated lemon on his head, Bruce Logan and Our Man Tony at 4th Street Recording in Santa Monica.

Steve with his electric banjo opening for Third Eye Blind

Analog recording gear at A&M Studios where The Uninvited mixed
their self-titled Atlantic album.

JT, Bill and Thom Panunzio at Fantasy Studios in Berkeley, CA.

Snow packed and burnt trailer.

Freezing our balls off somewhere in Middle America.

The Gnome in New Orleans with a Mississippi river boat.

The Gnome next to the Mutual of Omaha building in Omaha.

The Gnome on a bass rig in Phoenix, AZ.

DID YOU ENJOY THIS BOOK?

You can help make a difference for the author by showing your support!

Reviews are the most powerful tool in an author's arsenal when it comes to getting attention for their books. Honest reviews help bring the attention of other readers and spread the word so more people can enjoy the stories authors have to tell.

If you enjoyed this book, please consider taking a minute or two to leave a review on any of your sites.

We appreciate your support!

Acknowledgments

This book would not exist without the love, support and advice of John "JT" Taylor, whose willingness to do foolish things with his brother led to every adventure in this manuscript.

Massive love and thanks to the original rhythm section of Bill Cory and Bruce Logan, who brought the thunder every single night.

I would also like to thank all my other brothers who lent their amazing musical talents to the band including Clay Goldstein, Ladd Story, Eddie Ecker, Alex Fuller, John Messier and Tony Guiliano. They say if you're the best musician in the group, you're playing the wrong band. I was *always* in the right band.

Special love and gratitude to my beautiful wife, Mia Taylor, who not only gave a happy ending to the book but lived through the long hours of its creation while I was distracted, moody, nostalgic and steeped in self-doubt.

No acknowledgment section would be complete without massive props to Tony Medley, AKA Our Man Tony, who kept the wheels from falling off years and years.

Sam Helmi, our photographer, announcer, chef and hotelier was promised the Moon but ended up with a small rock – and our endless gratitude. We love you Sam.

To my early readers including Ellen Taylor, Marnie Green, Annemarie Gjestson and Raven Eckman your advice, insight and grammatical knowledge make this work readable! Thank you all so much.

To Meaghan Hurn and everyone at Hurn Publishing, who work tirelessly supporting the dreams of others, thank you for believing!

And finally, much love and gratitude to Mom and Dad, who taught me to go for it - no matter what

About The Author

As a musician, Steven V. Taylor has recorded 9 albums, two charting singles, and his music has been featured on some of TV's biggest hits including *Melrose Place, Beverly Hills 90210,* and *Party of Five,* along with several major motion pictures including HBO's *Bronx Tale, The Commandments* and *North Beach.* His band The Uninvited has played over 5,000 shows, sharing the stage with a host of rock legends from Cheap Trick to Blues Traveler.

Before starting down his musical path, Steven was interested in career opportunities in the field of Piracy. In pursuit of a swashbuckling life, he attended the California Maritime Academy, graduating with a Third Mate's license. After college he worked in the sub-zero temperatures of the Arctic, sailing on oil rig supply boats in the Bering Sea, and spent time on a dilapidated oil tanker on the Eastern Seaboard, but none of it came close to the romanticized pirate lifestyle he envisioned as a child.

Finally, in the late 1990's, Taylor realized his pirate dream – not as a sailor, but as a touring musician:

"You roll into town, burn the house to the ground, grab the money and get the hell out before the cops show up."

On the road he met the girl of his dreams, made a couple of

tiny pirates, and settled in Northern California. Though slightly more domesticated, he and The Uninvited still venture out on raids from time to time.

For more information on The Uninvited, visit www.Uninvited.com

Instagram: @official_uninvited_band

Need more Steve? Visit: www.StevenVTaylor.me

Book Club Questions

1. What was your initial reaction to the book? Did it hook you immediately or did it take time to develop and bring you in?
2. What was surprising about the facts contained in this book?
3. What was your favorite quote/passage?
4. What made the setting unique or important? Could the story have taken place anywhere?
5. Did you pick out any themes throughout the book?
6. How credible/believable did you find the narrator? Do you feel like you got the true story?
7. How did the characters change throughout the story? Did your opinion of them change?
8. How did the structure of the book effect the story?
9. Which character did you relate to the most, and what was it about them that you connected with?
10. How did you feel about the ending? What did you like, what did you not like, and what do you wish had been different?
11. Did the book change your opinion or perspective on anything? Do you feel different now than you did before you read it?
12. The book is being adapted into a movie, who would you want to see play what parts?
13. What is your impression of the author?

ABOUT THE EDITOR

A New Look On Books
Raven Eckman, Editor

Raven is a freelance editor by night and fangirl at every other available opportunity.

She always knew books were her passion, well after her grandmother's challenge to read a book a day and obtained her B.A. in English with a concentration in Creative Writing from Arcadia University.

Currently, she is drowning in her TBR list, revising her second WIP, and expanding her freelancing business-all while looking for more bookish things to get involved with.

She is active on Twitter, Instagram and sometimes Facebook when she remembers.

Editor Links:
Website: https://anewlookonbooks.com/
Twitter: @rceckman
Instagram: @anewlookonbooks

ABOUT THE PUBLISHER

Hurn Publications is the proud publisher of great writers and
gifted storytellers, beloved books and eminent works.
We believe that literature can fuel the imagination and guide the
soul. There is a book on our shelves for every reader, and we relish
the opportunity to publish across every category and interest with
the utmost care, attention to diverse inclusion and enthusiasm.

Find your next great read: www.hurnpublications.com

HP Newsletter Signup

Signing up for our newsletter gets you **Book Reviews, Books On Tour, Cover Reveals, Giveaways** and **Book Sales** delivered right to your inbox.
Stay up to date in the Indie Publishing world!

Link: https://www.subscribepage.com/hurnpublications

Copyright 2021 by Steven Taylor

To request permission, contact the publisher at Publish@HurnPublications.com
Paperback: 978-1-955547-30-7

eBook: 978-1-955547-31-4

Hardback: 978-1-955547-29-1

Audiobook: 978-1-955547-32-1

Library of Congress Control Number: 2021943123

First Edition: September 2021

Edited by: Raven Eckman of A New Look On Books

Cover Designer: Diana TC, https://triumphbookcovers.com

Hurn Publications | Harlingen, TX

www.hurnpublications.com

CPSIA information can be obtained
at www.ICGtesting.com
Printed in the USA
FSHW021836190821

9 781955 547307